T0271488

BIS Publishers
Building Het Sieraad
Postjesweg 1
1057 DT Amsterdam
The Netherlands
T +31 (0)20 515 02 30
bis@bispublishers.com
www.bispublishers.com

ISBN 978 90 6369 579 8

The Umami Strategy

Stand out by mixing business
with experience design

Aga Szóstek, PhD

BISPUBLISHERS

For Łukasz, always!

For Andrzej,
the best second father a girl can have

For my students
who always keep me on my toes

In the memory of
Kees Overbeeke (1952–2011)

LIST OF CONTENTS

Practical Tools for Your Umami Strategy

PART III   Keeping the Umami Mindset

Foreword

Unique. It's a word that stirs emotions from joy to fear. Joy at being truly your best self. Fear at standing out from the crowd.

Yet, those rare individuals and brands that own their uniqueness and dare to put their stamp on the world are the ones we remember. Elon Musk. Steve Jobs. Disney. Southwest Airlines. People say, "There will never be another…(fill in the blank)", and they are right.

Many authors want to help you become "the next…(fill in the blank)," but I'm excited to say that Aga Szostek wants to help you become so much more than a pale copy of someone else. Blending insights at the leading-edge of experience strategy with detailed implementation tactics, Aga shows you how to think and act your way to your unique experience. Borrowing the culinary concept of umami, she shows you how to blend the ingredients of your business to create and sustain something truly unique and memorable.

Packed with delectable stories, broad scholarship, bold insights, and practical techniques this book is a five star four course meal. It will leave you full, energised, and ready to act.

I think the best compliment you can give to a non-fiction author is to say, "Your book sounds like you." This book sounds like Aga. A keen observer and synthesiser of the world, she's brought her whole self into this book and lived her umami strategy in its pages. A perfect blend of emotion, functionality, aesthetics and fun, this is the experience cookbook you'll reach for again and again.

April K. Mills
author of *Everyone is a Change Agent*

Introduction

"Let us think the unthinkable, let us do the undoable,
let us prepare to grapple with the ineffable itself,
and see if we may not eff it after all."

Douglas Adams,
Dirk Gently's Holistic Detective Agency

It may seem as though everything has already been written when it comes to creating a successful business strategy. Yet, one is necessary if you want to stand out on the market, keep on being loved and admired by your customers, and shape a word of mouth about your business. For that, you might find yourself looking for a new way to define your own powerful, and highly actionable, experience strategy.

Why do you need an experience strategy? Although you might not fully realise it yet, your clients likely buy experiences from you, rather than services or goods. In years to come, experiences will become the cornerstone of generating unique market value. These experiences are something you should turn to your strategic advantage.

I was still a PhD student when a friend asked me, "What is an experience?". When I joined the business world almost a decade later,

I found that this question matters in business too. It shows how our perceptions, fleeting momentary glimpses, build us over time as personalities, as people who remember and tell stories. What we experience determines the impressions we walk away with, influences our choices, and shapes the stories we share with others about the products and services we encounter. These stories become the word of mouth—the most powerful marketing tool today.

Just knowing what your customers say about you can tell you what stories you might want to amplify, and which to extinguish.[1] The crucial next step is to ask if there a way to shape those stories. The good news is that there is. To influence customers' stories you need a strategy that consists of three things: a powerful experience vision, the 'edges'[2] (those qualities that will make you stand out from the competition), and a set of relevant metrics. As simple as this may sound, implementing such a strategy raises practical questions: how should you collect customer stories? What are the edges for? How do you define a truly actionable experience metrics? In this book, you will find the answers to all these questions.

Why is the word umami in the title of a book about strategy? Let me confess: I love cooking. After years of practical fascination with it, I got curious about the science behind how taste works. As you may know, there are basic flavours – sweet, salty, bitter and sour – that balance the taste of the food we eat. For ages, we believed these were the four elements we believed covered all bases. As it turns out, though, there is one more flavour that makes everything taste better. It is called umami and it means "tastiness" or "deliciousness". Umami was discovered in Japan about a century ago but has only recently attracted global attention. It is the fifth flavour that joins sweet, sour, salty and bitter, and elevates them to the next level. This is why so many people love pizza with its blend of tomatoes, mushrooms and parmesan cheese – seductive, potent and full of umami. This is the missing piece, the next level, the fifth element of yum.

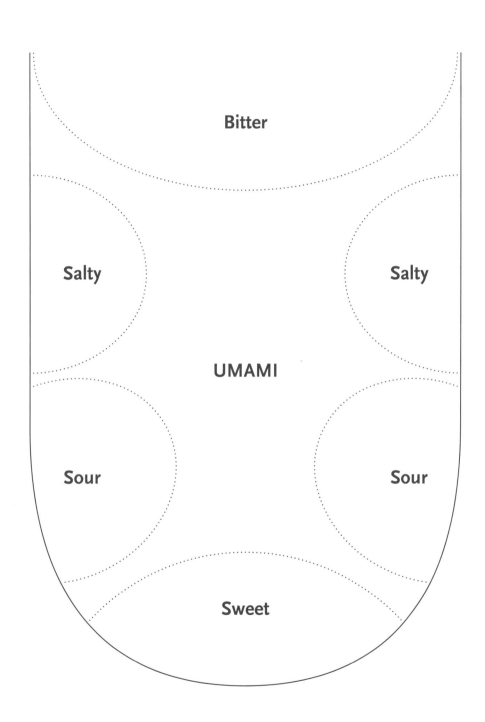

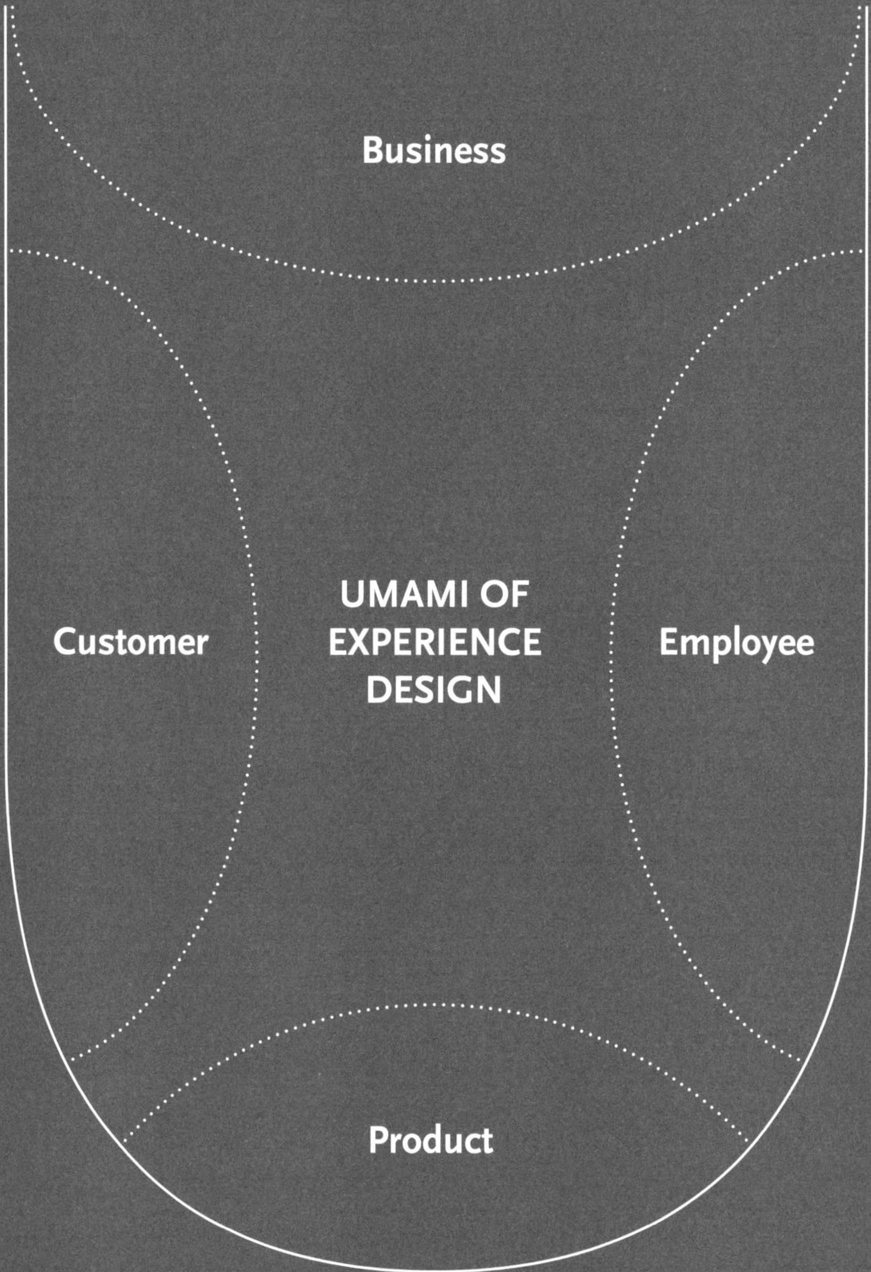

Business

Customer

**UMAMI OF
EXPERIENCE
DESIGN**

Employee

Product

When we look at the world of business, we often also stop at the four basic elements deemed to be strategic: business, product, customers and employees[3]. You might imagine that this is all you need, yet something is missing: the umami of experience that can take your offering all the way from adequate to unforgettable. It is the delicate yet persistent taste that makes people want to have more of it – for it to become irresistible pizza, if you will.

This book is the product of almost 20 years of blending academic and industrial research with business. For as long as I can remember, I have been interested in combining the worlds of technology, design and people. This led me to my Master's degree in User System Interaction, my PhD and work in a range of industrial research labs, including Philips Research, Océ Technologies research (today Canon) and Google. I have spent the last 10 years working on the business side of delivering a wide variety of experiences to customers. I have collaborated with service companies, manufacturers, food and drink producers, hospitality providers, national parks and local governments. I also spent five years with Play, a Polish telecoms company that challenged three market incumbents and became number one in what was seen as a seemingly fully saturated market. There, I helped with the definition and implementation of their experience strategy. It was the most fertile environment for testing and experimenting with many of the concepts described here; concepts that I later polished, tested and refined with other clients.

The uniqueness of this book lies in the way it offers you a way to define a powerful and highly actionable approach to an experience strategy. It will allow you to think of and implement an experience strategy that will ignite your business, help you stand out and make you become truly loved by your customers. I've seen it work, and I can't wait for you to see it work too. In these pages you will find both the reasoning and the practical tools you need. They aid you to create a company that is known for having worked out the secret sauce: a great experience customers just can't get enough of, and are happy to tell others about.

The Cloths of Heaven

Had I the heaven's embroidered cloths,
Enwrought with golden and silver light,
The blue and the dim nd the dark cloths
Of night and light and the half-light;
I would spread the cloths under your feet:
But I, being poor, have only my dreams;
I have spread my dreams under your feet;
Tread softly because you tread on my dreams.

W. B. Yeats

PART I

Discovering the Competitive Advantage of Experiences

CHAPTER ONE

The Experiencing and Remembering Self

Have you ever made a list of the best meals you have ever eaten? Here's one of mine. Years ago, my husband and I went to Kenya and spent a few days in Mombasa. We heard that there was a great restaurant there and we thought, "Why not try it out?" We were rather unaware of the dangers of walking the streets of the city, so instead of catching a cab we decided to stroll there. It was a hot afternoon. The pavements soon disappeared, so we walked on the side of a dusty street, passing ever shabbier huts. The smells of the local food stalls were bringing sweetness to the air. The shops offered everything you could imagine. It was a truly unadulterated insight into life off the beaten track in Mombasa.

We had heavily underestimated the distance, so after almost two hours of brisk walking we finally arrived at the gate of the restaurant. You might imagine that our appearance was far from elegant. We looked like we had arrived there by coincidence rather than on purpose. Also, there was no pavement outside, only a barrier for cars. The guard gave us a queer look as we asked him to open it for us. Slightly worried whether we were appropriately dressed, we arrived at the restaurant entrance. A flawless waiter welcomed us as if we were just the guests he had been waiting for the entire afternoon, and led us to a table with an amazing view of Port Reitz.

The restaurant was almost empty at that hour. Two other couples were sitting on the other side of the bright, spacious room. The windows were open and the breeze from the water felt really refreshing. We ordered shrimps and a bottle of wine, and sat there watching the sun setting over the old city. The peacefulness of this place was magical. We had not even once considered we might not have been "the right guests" for this establishment. As it darkened, we realised we should get on our way if we were to make it back to the hotel, preferably not on foot this time.

Before departing, my husband went to the bathroom. A few minutes later, he came back grinning and said, "You need to go too. And look at the walls as you walk there." Intrigued, I went. There was a long, wide corridor, full of pictures in simple, elegant frames. I looked at the first one and gasped with shock. It was a picture of the former Dutch Queen, Beatrix. Next to that was a picture of the British ambassador. The walls were a gallery of photographs of kings, queens, presidents and other famous people who had dined here at some point in time. No wonder there was no pavement leading to this place. Most likely, except for us, no one had ever walked in on foot.

As we departed, laughing at ourselves for being so ignorant, we realised, "Nobody has given us the slightest indication that we didn't belong there. We were treated in the exact same amazing way as any other guest who was there. What an experience that was!" What, do you think, did the word "experience" mean in this context? Was it the food we tasted? Was it the way we were treated? Or was it an aggregated memory of this visit that I've just shared with you?

The qualities of experience
Close your eyes for a moment and think about the last time you visited your favourite café.
- Where did you arrive there from?
- Who were you with?
- What mood were you in?
- What was the weather like outside?
- Was it crowded or empty?
- Where did you sit? Did you like that place?
- What did you order?
- How were you treated by the staff?
- What did you do? Chatted with friends? Maybe read something? Talked on the phone? Worked?
- Where were you heading afterwards?
- If you were to name that experience what would you call it?
- If you were to compare it to another visit to that café, what would be the difference?

The first important quality of experiences is that they are contextual.[4] Imagine you have just entered your favourite café. The waiter smiles and immediately brings you your favourite coffee. You feel noticed and treated as a valuable guest. Now imagine it again, but this time the waiter ignores you for 15 minutes, comes to you with an unhappy face and treats you as a terrible nuisance. Most likely, you feel annoyed, realise that the coffee is not as good as it used to be and consider whether you want to come back. It is the same place, the same drink, but what a different context to your experience.

You also need to realise that experiences are dynamic. They consist of a string of events rather than just a single one. Consider once again the visit to your favourite café. You just got there cold and wet, as the weather is a typical Northern European November day. You haven't seen the sun for a week and your energy level is low. You see that your favourite table is occupied by some youngsters who chat loudly over empty cups. You choose another table, sit down, and impatiently wait for someone to offer you a hot cup of your favourite flat white. Nobody comes for the next 10 minutes and you get even more annoyed. You are about to stand up and leave when a waiter comes and takes your order. Think of the thoughts going through your head at this moment.

Suddenly, the door opens and your best friend is standing there. She smiles and hugs you warmly. She just got great news and is keen to share it with you. As you both order another coffee, she notices the sad face of the waiter. She enquires about it and you learn that his dog just fell sick and he can't stop worrying about it. You feel deep sympathy and immediately forget the previous situation. The gruesome afternoon turns into a lovely evening and you remember this experience as great. Although you were not happy about what was happening at all times, at the end of the day you think of it as a nice experience. So, what do we mean when we talk about experience? I suggest that we use the definition proposed by the Nobel Prize winner Daniel Kahneman and his research partner, Jason Riis. They talk about two different perspectives on how we define the experiences in our lives: the perspective of the Experiencing Self and that of the Remembering Self.[5]

The Experiencing and Remembering Self

In 2012, a Kickstarter campaign had astonishing success.[6] It was an idea for a camera called Memoto designed to log every moment of your life.★ Many people bought it to create a surrogate memory outside of their own head.[8] This small device was designed to capture the perceptions of the Experiencing Self: the part of us that records what happens as we live our lives and then quickly forgets about most of these moments.★★ Poetically speaking, the Experiencing Self lives each moment so that it barely has time to exist. Pause for a moment to notice what is going on with you right now: your mental state, physical comfort and other subjective aspects of your present experience. Most likely you won't remember any of it in an hour. For the Experiencing Self, the experience can be seen as a chunk of time we went through with sounds and smells, and the feelings, actions and motives attached to it.[9]

There is another part of us though, called the Remembering Self. It is a powerful storyteller, which determines how we assess the events that happen to us, including our interactions with products and brands. The Remembering Self keeps score, maintains records and judges our lives according to how satisfactory they are. This is the part of ourselves that ultimately determines whether we are happy about a given service or a product, or not.

These two selves are responsible for our decision-making processes. Yet, the stories both selves tell are very different from each other. Imagine that you are asked to rate how much you enjoy spending time with your kids as compared to grocery shopping.[10] American economist Thomas Juster, and his colleague Frank Stafford, from the institute for Social Research at the University of Michigan, asked that question in one of their studies. As you might imagine, the majority of people rated the time spent with their children much

★   Today, Memoto is called Narrative Chip and is a really tiny camera[7].
★★   If you think about it, you captured about 20 000 such moments in your wak-
     ing day, which adds up to 500 million moments if you were to live up to
     the age of 70.

higher than the time they spent shopping. Their Remembering Selves wanted to believe that raising kids must be more enjoyable than buying bread and butter. But another study, where parents were asked to rate their day-to-day experiences with their children, demonstrated that their life satisfaction dropped when the children were born and that it recovered once they left home.[11] So, it seems that having kids is a somewhat mixed pleasure. Our Experiencing Selves see how difficult it can be at times but, on the other hand, viewed through the perspective of the Remembering Self, once the less happy times pass, you remember the joyful moments of the kid taking their first steps or hugging you after returning from holiday, rather than the daily struggles that raising children incurred. So, which Self should we focus on when designing experiences? Both of them. The sweet spot for experience design lies in creating moments of life both worth living and worth remembering.

CHAPTER TWO
The Nature of Expectations

Think of your next holiday. How great will it be? Terence R. Mitchell from the School of Business Administration at the University of Washington ran a study about people's expectations toward vacation enjoyment.[12] He showed that we tend to have a rather rosy view when thinking about upcoming events. For example, we imagine that our holidays will be much nicer than they typically are. The funny thing is that, after the holidays are over, we tend to remember them much more positively than when we were experiencing them in real time.[13],[*] So, it seems that our Remembering Self, together with the Experiencing Self, decide, even before anything happens, what sort of experience we will have. In other words: we envision what memory we will have at the end of a certain event. Daniel Kahneman calls this phenomenon the "creation of future past memories", which is nothing more than a process of forming expectations to anticipate an upcoming experience.

The cognitive illusion
Every now and then, we all wonder what it would be like to have another job, in another city, with another boss. For example, many people dream of living in California. They expect that Silicon Valley will offer them great professional opportunities, together with sunny weather all year long. How often do these expectations turn out to be true? Princeton University scholars, David Schkade and

[*]   Mitchell further points out that such a rosy view could have both positive and negative implications and concludes: "Rosy retrospection, for example, may suggest some reasons or circumstances where people learn less from experience than they could or should. Constantly rewriting the past in a favourable light may mean we don't adjust to the demands of the future."

Daniel Kahneman, asked almost 2000 students (half of them studying in Ohio and half in California) about their overall life satisfaction.[14] Then they asked how much happier or less happy they would be if they moved to the respective states. They were able to show that the relative advantages of California or disadvantages of the Midwest mattered a lot when a resident of one region considered the possibility of living in the other. But when students answered a question about their life satisfaction, their experience of living in either state was, in fact, quite similar. Schkade and Kahneman suspected that someone might actually decide to move to California in the mistaken belief that this would make them happier, which proves that we may not be such good judges of how our expectations match reality as we think we are.

Expectations are, in fact, a cognitive illusion—we are comparing the ideal to the real world. This illusion compels us to predict future events to be more extreme than those we actually end up experiencing.[15] When it comes to future interactions with a brand, we fall prey to this illusion too. This phenomenon is called "prospection" and it means that people are able to predict the pleasurable consequences of events they have never experienced. "We know that chocolate pudding would taste better with cinnamon than dill, that it would be painful to go an hour without blinking or a day without sitting, that winning the lottery would be more enjoyable than becoming paraplegic—and we know these things not because they've happened to us in the past, but because we can close our eyes, imagine these events, and pre-experience their hedonic consequences in the here and now."[16] Imagine, for example, that you are asked to drive a luxury car you always dreamt about driving. What would your expectations of this possible experience be? Do you see yourself speeding through the streets, the sound of the engine whirring through the air, the feel of the leather on your skin, and the envious looks of passers-by as you glide past?

When you analyse this experience from the perspective of the Experiencing Self, your actual momentary joy when driving the car of your dreams will likely be much lower than what you envisioned and will remember afterwards. It is because your Experiencing Self doesn't much care what model of car you drive, it is keeping you safe and making you think about when you should fill your tank next. The much bigger impact on how you perceive this experience comes from your life circumstances, which are rooted outside of the experience itself. In other words, if you are afraid of driving or generally unhappy with your life, having a chance to drive an amazing car is not going to make you feel any happier than driving a car that you would normally drive.[17] The much more critical aspect of your experience is actually *where* you are going, rather than how you are getting there. If you are heading for a dinner with your friends, you will perceive the drive to be much more pleasant than if you are driving to a dentist. And once you look back at the experience of driving the car of your dreams, your memory of it will most likely be much better than the reality of it was, simply because your Remembering Self wants you to remember it as an event worth experiencing in the first place.

Shaping expectations

When we combine our experiences with the stories we hear from others, these stories come together to form expectations.[18] Why is this the case? Karl Friston, a renowned neuroscientist and one of the pioneers of the predictive coding hypothesis at University College London, observed that our brains are constantly analysing data in order to allocate sufficient energy for future activities. In other words, we collect "feedforward" signals, which we consider newsworthy, something we think we should pay attention to and deal with accordingly.[19]

Lisa Feldman Barrett, professor of psychology and neuroscience at Northeastern University, says that one of the important sources of such predictions (among other aspects, such as, for example, our bodily signals) are our past experiences, but as you might imagine, word of mouth is another source of information fuelling our predictive capabilities. If I recall the last time I went to my stylist, my brain knows it doesn't have to store too much energy for the next visit as the experience is, overall, pleasant and relaxing. On the other hand, my past experiences with Amazon Sellers support indicate to my brain that this activity is likely going to cost me a lot of energy. In situations like this, the first defence of our brains is to try to discourage us from going into the negative experience. The brain knows that the use of energy will be costly and "thinks" that we might be better off if we avoid it, hence our reluctance to take the first step, like picking up the phone to make an unpleasant call. Once the brain realises we will pursue the negative interaction anyway, it secures enough energy for us to survive the battle, such as, for example, pumping us with adrenaline (this is why we feel the emotion of dread or anger even before that interaction begins). So, in a way, the Remembering Self has one job — to provide the brain with enough information to make the best decision regarding the amount of energy needed for a certain activity that the Experiencing Self is about to go through.

Unfortunately, the Remembering Self is not the best predictor of what will happen because it is prone to the optimism bias.★ Optimism bias causes us to believe that we are more likely to experience a positive event, or less likely to experience a negative event, compared to other people. For example, smokers believe they are less likely to contract lung cancer than other smokers, first-time bungee jumpers believe they are less at risk of injury than other jumpers, and traders think they are less exposed to potential losses in the markets compared to other traders.[21] When we are imagining our future, our Remembering Selves have a tendency to overestimate the potential for positivity (like believing you will be treated better than others) and underestimate the potential for negativity (such as being less likely to have a drinking problem).[22] In other words, we imagine our futures in the form of positively biased scenarios. For example, when you think about who you will be in 10 years, you are more likely to see

★   It is important to note that the concept of optimism bias was recently criticised in many ways. In an important paper related to this critique[20], the authors conclude the following: "Five experiments tested for optimistic belief updating through the use of a variety of events (both positive and negative) and via a number of analyses. Overall, no evidence for optimistic updating was observed. The results of Sharot and colleagues thus do not provide additional evidence in favour of a general human optimistic tendency. Furthermore, even if subsequent research does point to the universality of unrealistic optimism, the underlying mechanisms and neurobiology supporting the phenomenon remain unknown."

yourself as better-off, smarter, and still good looking rather than poor, forgetful and aged. We expect to receive higher starting salaries and more job offers than we end up getting. We tend to underestimate how long a project will take to complete and how much it will cost. We predict deriving greater pleasure from a vacation than we subsequently get and we anticipate encountering more positive events in an upcoming month than we end up experiencing.

We also update our beliefs about the future more in response to positive than to negative information and we maintain this bias even when we are faced with contradicting evidence. Tali Sharot, professor of cognitive neuroscience at University College London, showed this in the following experiment. She and her team asked a group of participants to estimate their chances of encountering serious negative events in their lifetime, like serious illness or being assaulted. Once the participants had their numbers, the researchers showed the statistical probability of facing such events. For the vast majority, the real numbers were much higher than what they predicted. The participants were then asked to estimate the likelihood of experiencing these events once more. Oddly enough, it seemed that the statistics didn't have much influence on changing their beliefs. People who gave more optimistic estimates than the statistical data stuck to their initial estimates. Furthermore, the people who were initially more pessimistic than the numbers indicated tended to adjust their initial estimates to meet the (more positive) statistical data. It seems that facts have an impact on us only if they help to improve our odds. Otherwise, our optimism is resistant to change even when we are faced with reality.

At the biological level, the optimism bias stems from the activation of the amygdala (the part of our emotional system mainly responsible for processing salient features of surroundings that could be life-threatening) and of the rostral anterior cingulate cortex, which takes care of our emotional regulation.★ What is crucial to know though: our optimism increases with uncertainty. We are far too optimistic in situations

---

★   According to the biologist Ajit Varki, evolution of humans might have come to a halt without this very bias as it makes us try new things and not get discouraged by failure.[23]

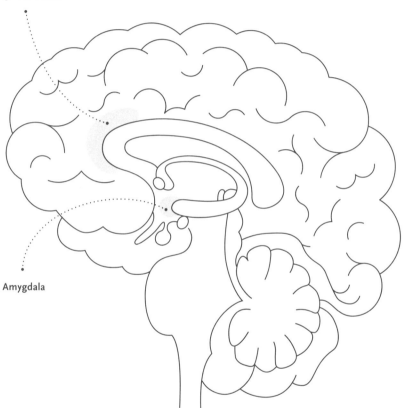

**Rostral Anterior
Cingulate Cortex**

Amygdala

bearing the greatest unknowns. According to Dominic D. P. Johnson, a professor of International Relations at St Antony's College, Oxford, and James H. Fowler, a professor of Political Science and Medicine at the University of California, in the scientific journal *Nature*, being an optimist has a number of advantages.[24] It helps us be ambitious, increases our morale, makes us persistent and even improves our credibility when we are bluffing. It can be compared to generating a self-fulfilling prophecy in which exaggerated confidence actually increases our probability of success.[25] But it can also be hazardous. Underestimating risk can lead to being less cautious and actually promote engaging in harmful behaviours.

At the cognitive level, the optimism bias is connected to our perception of having control over our lives. We believe that if we truly have the ability to command our future, we have the power to steer it towards the positive scenarios and away from the negative ones.[26] Professor Martin Seligman, a director of the Penn Positive Psychology Centre at the University of Pennsylvania, suggests that (once we figure out that we have no control over our circumstances) we tend to become depressed.[27] Optimism bias also influences how we build our expectations towards different brands and how imprecise these expectations tend to be. So, the good news for any business is that this very bias will keep us hoping that good experiences will happen, even if the insights from word of mouth or our previous experiences prove the contrary. But it also means that most customer expectations might be too optimistic and therefore unattainable and difficult for your brand to fulfil.

The zone of tolerance

Customer expectations could be viewed on a scale that ranges from desired to adequate.[28] Our optimistic hopes are expressed on the side of the desired experience, while what is adequate is what we are willing to settle for. Arun Parasuraman, Leonard Berry and Valarie Zeithaml, researchers from Texas A&M University, called this difference the "zone of tolerance".★

★   The zone of tolerance can vary from customer to customer, and from one situation to the next.

The adequate end of the scale reflects the lowest possible level of experience that we are willing to accept before we deem something unacceptable, and start looking for alternatives. If the experience you deliver is worse than that which your customers see as adequate, they will be disappointed and their Remembering Self will make sure that they avoid your brand in the future. Even if these customers remain (because they are bound by a contract, for example), you begin to cultivate what are called "reluctant customers" — who will stay with you only as long as they have an obligation towards you.

If your brand stays within the Zone of Tolerance, you will be seen as reasonable but nothing special (this is actually where most companies are positioned). Your customers will enter a transactional relation with your brand, which can be expressed through the statement "value for money". It represents a transactional relationship, a relationship in which your customers remain until a better option shows up on the horizon. But, if the experience you deliver exceeds what was seen as desired, your customers will encounter a feeling of positive surprise and they will be both more likely to commit emotionally to your brand and to share the story of this experience with others.★

★   Based on this model, the authors of this concept developed a tool called Servqual that measures service quality as perceived by customers, used in industries such as automotive, insurance or repair.

CHAPTER THREE

The Experience Equation

We have looked into three elements of experience so far: our expectations as well as what our Experiencing Self and Remembering Self notice. These elements create a simple equation, where our memories of experiences are formed by the impressions of the Experiencing Self contrasted with the expectations your customers held when they entered the interaction with your brand.★

$$\frac{\text{impressions of the Experiencing Self}}{\text{expectations}} = \begin{array}{c} \text{memories of} \\ \text{the Remembering Self} \end{array}$$

EXPERIENCE EQUATION

This equation tries to reflect the chemical reactions of our brains. When something sort-of-okay happens, our body produces a small amount of dopamine, so our pleasure levels rise only slightly and our brain (our Remembering Self) doesn't find such an experience worth noting for future reference. A similar reaction happens with a sort-of-not-okay experience. This time our body produces a small amount

★   You might recognise the elements of the Experience Equation as being close to those of the Satisfaction Equation.[29] Indeed, this method of measuring satisfaction, which used to be popular in the 2000s, can be compared to what I propose here. However, the Experience Equation broadens the ways in which you can look at what builds customers' emotional involvement and loyalty.

of adrenaline and cortisol, the hormones responsible for the evolutionary fight-or-flight response. Our brain might fairly easily rebuff such an event as non-threatening and make us forget it as soon as the moment passes. But if the experience is either surprisingly positive or surprisingly negative, our body pumps up the chemicals in our blood, putting our brain on high alert. While a high level of dopamine gives us a rewarding feeling, adrenaline is responsible for increasing our perception of threat. So, our brain makes our Remembering Self record these events in the form of a memory that is stored to help us make future choices.

Overpromising

Hotel experiences can provide good material for comparison in this matter. Think of two hotels — hotel A and hotel B. Hotel A is described in the following way:

"Situated in X, hotel A provides a terrace. All rooms boast a flatscreen TV with cable channels and a private bathroom. Both free WiFi and private parking are available on site. All rooms in the hotel are fitted with a coffee machine. All units include a desk. A continental breakfast is served each morning at the property. We speak your language."

The pictures show a contemporary space giving an impression of a boutique hotel hidden away from the tourist area. So imagine your reaction, when, upon arrival, you find yourself in a motel rather than a hotel, with the terrace being an entry to the rooms, with no breakfast and no dedicated parking space. Most likely you'd feel cheated, experience a rush of adrenaline and your Experiencing Self would make sure that your Remembering Self marked this experience as disappointing. Why is this so?

The description of the accommodation built on your previous experiences with similar hotels and set your expectations. When you arrived, these expectations took a major hit compared to the reality you encountered. If it were just one or two things misaligned with how you imagined this hotel, you would see it perhaps not as your desired accommodation but as adequate. But as, so many things failed to live up to the description, your Experiencing Self had no other choice but to assess this as a disappointment.

Take a look at hotel B now. Before booking it, you were considering whether you should choose this place as the promise made through the description and the pictures felt somewhat factual. When you arrive, you see a space that is contemporary but cosy. The furniture is handmade and of amazing quality. The room doors open onto a little garden with running water. There is a terrace on the top floor with a little kitchenette. Chilled water and fruits are waiting on the table and next to them you find a booklet with recommendations for restaurants and local attractions. It feels like a little piece of paradise. In this case, your expectations are downplayed, so there is space left for positive surprise. This allows your Experiencing Self to feel a significant rush of dopamine that results in a great memory created by your Remembering Self.

I visited these two hotels some time ago. When staying at hotel B, I asked the owners why they didn't put more representative pictures on their site. They said, "If we overpromise, the best case scenario is that our guests will see that the place matches the pictures. In the worst case, they will be disappointed because they imagined more. We'd rather underpromise and overdeliver than the other way around." In this simple statement they summarised the quintessence of the experience equation: if you overpromise from the beginning you can only hope to live up to that promise. If you underpromise, you give yourself the space to exceed expectations and create a memory for the Remembering Self that your customers will want to share with others.

However, if you look around you can see the opposite happening. Marketing campaigns leap out at us from every corner, promising more and better. It seems that in the battle for attention, in which we aim to lock in the customer as quickly as possible. It is a rather shortsighted strategy because we soon find out that it is hard to live up to these promises. Not because companies don't want to, but because the optimism bias of their customers makes them inflate their expectations and companies then don't have sufficient resources to fulfil them. This is the moment when customers get disappointed. We will come back to this later.

First impressions count less than you think

There seem to be a few more myths about how an experience should be designed. One of these is, first impressions count. This belief often leads companies to spend excessive money and effort on creating a remarkable first impression. Supermarkets are a good example of this. They are often arranged so that the fruit and vegetable stalls and the bakery items are located at the front of the store. But when you arrive at the cash register, the shelves with the impulse purchase items, such as chewing gum and small packs of candies, rarely look attractive.

There is no question that first impressions are important. A study into the retail industry by Morpace, a market research firm, showed that a negative impression of the external appearance of a shop caused participants to avoid it.[30] More than two thirds of customers said they decided against visiting a business for the first time based on its external appearance. One half (52 percent) said they shunned a business altogether because it looked dirty from the outside. One third chose not to enter a business because it "didn't look like a place I would normally shop." Although those customers couldn't pinpoint specifically why they didn't want to shop there, it was something about the appearance that gave them pause.

The saying "first impressions count" seems to imply that these first impressions create a lasting impact. However, a large body of research in the field of behavioural economics tells us that first impressions aren't really that important in determining how we remember (and judge) an interaction with a brand. What, in fact, impacts our memories is most powerfully influenced by two things: how the experience felt when it was at its emotional peak (best or worst) and how it felt when it ended.[31] This rule is called the "peak-end rule".

Peak-end rule

The peak-end rule is another cognitive bias that impacts how we remember past events. Intense positive or negative moments (the "peaks") and the final moments of an experience (the "end") impact heavily on how our memories are shaped. In an interview for National Public Radio (NPR), Daniel Kahneman said, "Memory was

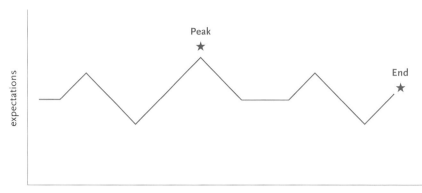

impressions of the Experincing Self

not designed to measure ongoing happiness, or total suffering. For survival, you really don't need to put a lot of weight on duration of experiences. It is how bad they are and whether they end well, that is really the information you need as an organism."[32]

Between 1993 and 2005, Kahneman ran a series of experiments analysing that rule.[33] In one experiment, he and his colleagues asked participants to hold their hand in cold water (a temperature of 14°C). In one version, participants were asked to keep their hand in the water for one minute. In the other, they held their hand in the cold water for 90 seconds, but over the last 30 seconds of the experiment, the temperature was slowly raised to 15°C. It was still painful but distinctly less so for most subjects.

After experiencing both conditions, participants were given a chance to indicate which procedure they would choose to repeat. From a theoretical perspective, it would make sense that they would select the shorter procedure. Yet, most of them selected the longer trial for the simple reason that they remembered more strongly how it ended than how it started. This phenomenon is called a "duration neglect" and it is a by-product of evolution. We didn't need to know for how long a wolf attacked us, we needed to know if it was a bad experience, and if it ended well. It was the information we needed in order to avoid another wolf attack, and thus the information our brain was wired to store.

On the other hand, our experiences are deeply determined by peak moments — "an altered state of consciousness characterised by euphoria, often achieved by self-actualising individuals."[34] A peak moment is a concept proposed by American psychologist, Abraham Maslow, who described them as "rare, exciting, oceanic, deeply moving, exhilarating, elevating experiences that generate an advanced form of perceiving reality, and are even mystic and magical."[35] Peak experiences can range from simple activities to intense events; however, it is not necessarily about what the activity is, but the feeling that is experienced during it.[36] As Chip and Dan Heath explore in their book *The Power of Moments: Why Certain Experiences Have Extraordinary Impact,* these feelings include:[37]

- elevation, which means moments of happiness that transcend the normal course of events, through sensory pleasures and surprise;

- pride, which indicate moments that capture us at our best, whether they be moments of achievement or moments of courage;

- insight, which are our *eureka* moments, which change our understanding of ourselves and the world, and give us a moment of sobering clarity;

- connection, which are moments of a social nature that give us the opportunity to connect with others.

What this means is that, within any given experience, some moments will always be more memorable than others. The value of these moments can have a profound impact on our lives and the way we perceive the world. "A single glimpse of heaven is enough to confirm its existence even if it is never experienced again," Maslow wrote. These moments might be difficult to pin down but they are the basis of a memory of any given experience. The peak-end bias suggests that, when designing experiences, it is more important to build a high emotional peak and a graceful ending than to reduce the number of low moments.[38] The impact of the peak-end rule can be further strengthen if both the peak and end moments carry a personal meaning.[39]

The experience curve

This rule of creating peak-end moments is well known in game design. Game producers know that in order to get people into a game, you need to start with a bang. Then you need to let people relax a little, otherwise their emotional arousal will be too high. Next, you should create a peak moment—a moment when you get them excited again. And you should finish strongly so they want to come back for more in the future.

Let's map the two hotel experiences through the lens of the Experience Curve.★ From the description on the hotel website, your expectations were high. Once you arrived, no parking lot was available. This was the first blow. The second came when you were given keys to your room by a bored concierge who didn't speak English. While getting to the room, you realised that this place was more of a motel than a hotel, with the advertised "patio" being just an entry to your room. Although the room itself was decent, the previous blows made you see it as worse than expected. The final blow came in the morning when you went looking for breakfast and there was none to be found. Think about this: the room itself wasn't uninviting. If it weren't for all the other moments, there was a chance you could have deemed this interaction as maybe not desirable but at least adequate. However, the overall experience, and especially the end of it, was so disappointing that your Remembering Self marked it as an example of an experience to avoid.

The opposite experience took place in hotel B. Your initial expectations were well managed through the description and pictures on the website that didn't showcase all its attractions. You knew that this place should be nice, but no more than that. Once you crossed

★   In the entertainment world this curve is called the Interest Curve but for the sake of consistency I am naming it the Experience Curve for the purpose of this book.

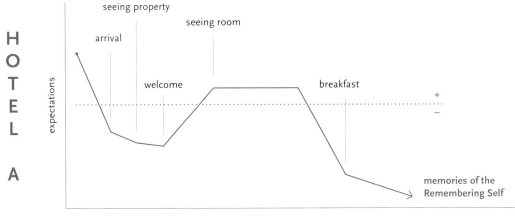

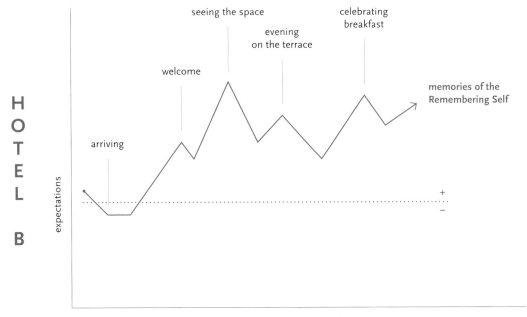

the threshold, you found yourself in a hidden oasis. The host welcomed you with coffee. He took time to answer all your questions and then he showed you to your room. Finally, he told you to ask for anything else you might need. In the morning you were served breakfast and spent two hours talking with your hosts who took a keen interest in you. As you were about to leave, you received a little parting gift, which was the cherry on the top. This is a great example of how to think of the experiences you create for your customers.

Once you become aware of the Experience Curve, you start seeing it in many places: in the three-act structure of movies; in the construction of pop songs (musical intro — verse — chorus — verse — chorus — solo — big finish); or in good videogames. Any experience that we see as memorable (be it scary, funny or engaging) has a structure that can be mapped out like this.

Some brands are very aware of the advantage of using the Experience Curve as their design framework. Have you ever wondered why there are inexpensive treats on offer at the exit of IKEA stores? This is their way of designing a great ending. But there is more. A number of moments along your shopping journey are well placed to offer you experiential peak points: the restaurant, the playground for kids, the "secret" shortcuts. This is all done so that you will remember the trip to their store and recall this memory whenever you consider shopping for home-related items. At Disney, every designer is asked to present 10 top moments of an experience they design. If they are not able to articulate these, their pitch is over. You might say that it is easy to design an Experience Curve for a relatively brief experience, like a visit to Disneyland, but how can you create one for a bank or a marketplace? Here's the trick: Experience Curves can be fractal.[40] You can design an overall Experience Curve that lasts over time and also design individual curves within its specific parts.

Professor Lisa Feldman Barrett further argues that our brain is a statistical engine that constantly categories everything that is going on with and around us in order to gain knowledge and to form a fairly reliable view of the world. We keep on looking for statistical regularities that can help us make informed decisions. So, as we go through an experience, we constantly evaluate it by subconsciously comparing it to any other similar experiences we recall (memories) in order to judge how good, insignificant or bad it is. We form hypotheses (expectations) about how this particular experience unfolds, we assess probabilities based on our previous knowledge (past experiences), integrate the evidence from the environment (the impressions of the Experiencing Self) and perform tests to see whether anything changes compared to our previous encounter. This is why it often happens that when you have an amazing experience and you repeat it later, you are not as impressed. It is like winning the lottery all over again. You need to be impressed repeatedly to keep on seeing an experience as a great one.[41],★ This is something we will look into in more depth in the last part of this book.

Experience is about building a long-lasting relationship

There is one more piece of research I would like to share. In the 1970s, two American psychologists, John Gottman and Robert Levenson, launched a study of romantic relationships that ran for over a decade.[42] They gave their participants 15 minutes to resolve a conflict, such as "which school should we send our kids to?" One aspect helped them predict with 90 percent accuracy whether a couple would stay together or divorce. The difference between happy and unhappy couples was the balance between positive and negative interactions during conflict. They called it the "magic ratio" and the balance was five to one. This means that for every negative interaction experienced during conflict, a marriage has to have at least five compensating positive interactions to remain stable and happy. "When the masters of marriage are talking about something important," Gottman said, "they may be arguing, but they are also laughing and teasing and there are signs of affection because they have made emotional connections." On the other hand, the unhappy couples engaged in fewer positive interactions to

★   There is an entire field dedicated to designing for experience named Positive Design, which gathers a variety of approaches, techniques and methods on how to create solutions that spark human flourishing.

compensate for their escalating negativity. If the positive-to-negative ratio during conflict was one-to-one or less, it became an indication that a couple was teetering on the edge of divorce.

The relationships we build with brands are not very different from the relationships we build with other people. And although perhaps the "magic ratio" may not be as big as in marriage, still the ratio between the positive and negative events needs to be significantly skewed towards the positive side. Remember the stay at hotel A? If you were only faced with the lack of the parking lot or the receptionist who didn't speak English but the other elements of this experience were positive, you would likely deem this experience as maybe not desirable but adequate. But, as the disappointments piled up, they were creating an overall negative memory of this visit. Likewise, with respect to the stay at hotel B, if you just liked the place but the hospitality of the owners was less than excellent, you would remember it as just one of the nice little hotels you visited in the past. Instead, as the positive experiences followed one after another, your memory of how amazing this place was became stronger and stronger. There might have been small disappointments, like waiting for the owner to arrive and open the door for you, but in sum they were overridden by all the great little moments you experienced throughout this stay. This is the exact same case with any other experience we live through, be it a shopping, dining or financial experience — we look for the positive emotional ratio in it. Once this ceases to be the case, we are inclined to look for another provider or, in other words, divorce a brand.

CHAPTER FOUR
The Myth of Rationality

Usually, if you ask anyone to list brands they truly admire, they will soon run into trouble. They might be able to list a few names they "sort of" like. They might have a list of brands they actively dislike. But thinking of a brand they feel emotionally attached to; that's hard. Since 2008, Havas, one of the largest communication companies in the world, has run a global study that utilises data from 1800 brands, across 31 markets and 22 industries to explore the ways in which brands "tangibly improve people's lives and the role they play in society."[43] They surveyed 350 000 consumers to determine those brands which consumers viewed as essential to their daily lives – as well as those they were indifferent about. The 2019 findings were daunting for many brands, as they showed that people wouldn't care if 77 percent of them disappeared overnight.

We have few feelings towards the brands that serve us. We see them through a utilitarian lens — they are either serving our particular needs or we abandon them. Our relationship with these brands is strictly transactional. It is a business deal where "you do something for me and I pay you for it". Not many emotions are involved. If your deal is no longer attractive to me, I will go somewhere else without thinking twice. Such a transactional approach is a legacy of the Industrial Revolution, which initiated the short-term pursuit of growth in earnings per share. It makes companies prioritise quick wins over focusing on the long-term process of building customer loyalty. One example of this is demonstrated by what has happened to customer service departments over recent years. The reason why customer service was created in the first place was to show customers that your brand cared about them. There were three reasons to show such care: fixing a problem, building a competitive advantage and transforming the experience of what it is to buy something. Yet today, customer service seems to be a system that couldn't care less about customers, with the ultimate goal of making people go away and figure out whatever they need on their own.

Many such departments experience the pressure to hire a cheaper workforce and to spend little time on individual conversations, which generates a conflict at the heart of the reason for their existence. This leads to disappointing your customers twice: once, when something goes wrong with your service, and the second time, when you show your disinterest in their problem. Remember the magic ratio? You will have to compensate for two negative points now. But somehow, for many companies it appears that it is more worthwhile to send customers away and keep on running after new customers, rather than dedicating time to make a valued customer happy.[44] There seems to be a conviction that somehow the next discount will compensate for that lack of concern. It is an approach based on the myth of human rationality, also called the theory of the homo economicus.

The myth of the homo economicus

Homo economicus characterises people as rational and focused on pursuing wealth for their own self-interest. The economic man is described as one who avoids unnecessary work by using rational judgment. The history of this term dates back to the 19th century, when John Stuart Mill defined the economic actor as one "who inevitably does that by which he may obtain the greatest amount of necessaries, conveniences, and luxuries, with the smallest quantity of labor and physical self-denial with which they can be obtained."[45] Mill followed other economists and philosophers, like Adam Smith and David Ricardo, who considered people to be rational, self-interested economic agents. Although there have been many critics of the theory of homo economicus, the idea that we predominantly act in our own self-interest remains a basis of today's economic thought, causing us (the people of Western civilisation) to believe that we are, above everything else, rational creatures.[46,47] We weigh pros against cons and, based on the result, we make decisions while having a firm grip on our emotions, which might be correct, but only to an extent.

When it comes to making choices, it would mean that it doesn't matter how something looks or makes us feel, that we make our choices based entirely on pragmatic considerations such as usability, reliability or functionality. But research shows this is not the case. Back in 2000, Noam Tractinsky, Adi Katz and Dror Ikar from Ben Gurion University in Israel ran a study to see what was more important: how usable something was or how aesthetically pleasing it looked. They designed four interfaces for an ATM machine. All interfaces offered the exact same functionality but they varied in both how usable and how good-looking they were.[48] Then they asked a number of participants to, first, declare whether they considered that both aesthetics and usability make their interaction with the ATM satisfactory or whether usability alone should be enough. Afterwards, the participants performed a task on a different ATM interface. At the end they were once more asked if they saw a correlation between the two qualities of the interface: usability and aesthetics. As you might have intuitively guessed, the more both beautiful *and* usable the system was, the more satisfactory the interaction itself was deemed to be. At this point it would be natural to assume that the level of usability affected participants' perceptions of how usable the system was, while the level of aesthetics impacted on their perception of the system's beauty. It turned out, however, that the interface that looked better was perceived as more usable, even if objectively this was not the case. It seemed that the sheer fact that something looked good meant its users expected it to work better.

Rather than having our perceptions influenced just by what we see and hear, we perceive things around us to a major extent through the lens of how we feel about them. If you think back to how expectations are formed — we envision how an interaction with an ATM machine will go and, based on that, we budget sufficient energy to undergo that interaction. Once we see a beautiful interface, our brain is positively surprised (as its expectations have been exceeded) and this positively impacts our perception of that interaction. It doesn't matter whether you choose between two snacks in the supermarket, two job offers, or judge how difficult it is to open a bank account, your brain will keep on guessing whether it is a good or bad decision based on how you feel about it. And what your affective side perceives, your rational side accepts as the truth.

The theory of the homo economicus dominated economic thought for many years, but it is time to put it to bed. At the beginning of the 20th century, a number of other philosophers and economists argued that the economic man is not a realistic model of human behaviour because economic actors do not always act in their own self-interest and are not always fully informed when making economic decisions. So, regardless of what you might have been taught, rationality is not the sole engine of our decision-making processes. Emotions have a large role to play in it. They play a role in crafting our emotional connection with brands and products as they underline both our expectations and our memories.

The way we make decisions
When it is time to buy a new apartment, do you just see the plans, read the specifications and then choose the most economical option? This would be the homo economicus way to decide. But making decisions is so difficult and complex that we are often at a loss as to how to make them.[49] We turn to reviews, opinions and our own feelings, so even when we think we are making a logical choice, more often than not we, in fact, base it on emotions. I would take it even further and suggest that (after the famous neuroscientist Antonio Damasio, a professor of psychology, philosophy and neurology, at the University of Southern California), if you can't feel emotions, you can't make decisions.[50]

The exercise of flipping a coin offers one example of the struggle between our rational and our emotional selves. Imagine that you are deciding between one of two jobs: a high-paying job at a prestigious firm that will require long hours; and a less stressful job at a less well-known company that provides more flexibility. You flip a coin, and the coin tells you to take the more prestigious job. But somehow you wish the coin had told you to take the other job, making you realise that you preferred the less prestigious, more flexible job all along. Swiss researchers, Mariela Jaffe, Leonie Reutner and Rainer Greifeneder, explain that flipping a coin makes the consequences of a decision more real, and therefore strengthens your feelings about it.[51] Once the coin flip has committed you to one option, you are able to realise which outcome you wanted all along.

Actually, many scientists assume that emotions are the dominant driver of most of our decisions.[52] They guide our everyday attempts at avoiding negative feelings (such as guilt, fear, regret) and increasing positive feelings (like pride, happiness, love), even when we lack awareness of these processes. And once the outcomes of our decisions materialise, we feel new emotions, provoking a new set of decisions.

A few years back, we asked customers how they think they make decisions when it comes to telecom services — what motivates them to choose one provider over another. Most of them declared that they were rational about it: they were driven by the value for money they were expected to spend. Next, we asked them to show us how they made one particular choice. For the first 15 minutes they tried to be pragmatic — they were comparing prices and the elements of the offering. But we made these offerings practically indistinguishable, as so often happens; in fact, there was no comparison between the two offers. What we observed was this: after satisfying their need for logical arguments, about 80 percent of participants grabbed their phones, called their family or friends, described each offering and what was "good" or "bad" about it, and took a final decision based on that information. It is the case because, as I mentioned before, making decisions is a complex and difficult process, in which we are not quite sure what our preferences are in the first place, so we keep creating simplification mechanisms that help us deal with that process.[53] Partial grounding of our decisions in our emotions and in the emotions of others is one of the most powerful mechanisms of all. And the more complex the decision, the more likely we are to fall back on our emotions to make it.[54]

The last 40 years of research about the influence of emotions on our decision-making processes show a number of aspects that are worth considering when creating business offerings.[55] Firstly, emotions are predictable drivers of decision making. If something makes us feel stressed, we will avoid it. If something makes us happy, we will strive to have more of it. Secondly, our emotions are deeply influenced by our implicit goals, things that we strive for personally. So, if your customers are sensitive to, for example, the environmental impact of your product or service, you can generate positive emotions in them by tapping into these needs. It is also important to remember that we are not homo economicus, nor are we the emotional beast—we combine our cognitive and emotional triggers to make decisions.

If emotions are so important when we are making a purchasing decision, you can only imagine how important they become once we start using a given service or product. Each time we enter such an interaction, our brain will want to predict how much effort it will cost us. If your brain assumes that a given interaction will be pleasurable, you experience satisfaction. If it assumes the opposite, you are going to feel dissatisfied. Experiencing a high level of satisfaction triggers the development of an emotional connection; as with food—if you like a certain dish, you are more likely to eat it again. But if the taste disagrees with you, you consider it as food that keeps you alive if you are starving but that you will ignore once you have another option. In other words, your relationship with everything that brings you satisfaction is likely to become emotional, while if you have to interact with something that is not particularly satisfactory, your relationship will remain transactional. You will use it as long as there is no better option available to you.

CHAPTER FIVE
Basics

There is a common misconception in marketing that satisfaction is an attribute of a brand, while in fact it is an attribute of us (the customer) and our interactions with the world around us.[56] In other words, when our interaction with the world around us is successful (with products and services being tools to that success), we feel satisfied. But our satisfaction is not with the product, or even the brand. We feel satisfied with ourselves. If we attribute part of this success to a product or service, we are likely to see it as valuable. If not, the opposite is the case.★ This satisfaction needs to be experienced on two levels: rational (pragmatic) and emotional (affective). And there is a threshold that separates them.

Experiential basics
Many companies think that, if they are present on the market and have something to offer, this alone will trigger people to join them. But this is not the case. You need to deliver on a number of aspects that address people's pragmatic needs before anyone considers giving you a chance.[57] All these pragmatic needs lie below the Umami Threshold—a point at which your customers decide whether they are willing to use your offering at all.[58] Imagine a new mobile phone provider entering your market. Even though, as a customer, you might like to support the underdog that is trying to disrupt the market, if the coverage is poor you are unlikely to switch. The same would be

★   Hence, it barely makes sense to ask anyone how satisfied they are with, let's say, a banking service, if they have never used it.

MOTIVATORS

affective value

Empathy   Fun   Engagement   Meaning

The Umami Threshold

Functionality   Reliability   Usability   Aesthetics

pragmatic value

BASICS

true of a new store in your neighbourhood with not enough groceries in stock for you to cook dinner. Or an amusement park with just one roller coaster. Some basic requirements need to be fulfilled, otherwise your brain predicts that the cost of use is going to be too high and discourages you from choosing that offering.

There is an ongoing discussion in the academic world about what qualities can be seen as such pragmatic aspects of an offering (I am going to call them "basics").[59] But it seems that four main qualities can be distinguished to form this category: functionality, reliability, usability and aesthetics. These are the aspects that must be met in order for you to meet the expectations of your customers and not disappoint them. Before we dive into the details of each of these aspects, it is important to remember that these are not human needs *per se*. They are the attributes that are fundamental for interaction to occur.[60] Imagine that you are waiting for a train and it is running late. How do you feel? Most likely, frustrated and annoyed. But if the train is on time, you are not going to jump around out of sheer joy. Your feelings are most likely neutral, as this is what you expected in the first place. This is due to the very nature of the basics — they can make you feel dissatisfied if they are absent, but they are not going to increase your satisfaction level if they are present. They are the necessary ingredients for an experience to take place but they are not those that make it stand out.

Functionality

Functionality is the most basic need that people have. Although this might seem like common sense, quite a number of companies, big and small, keep forgetting about this. Back when we were finishing our house, I decided I would love to have a fireplace. So I did what probably anyone would do: I went online and typed "small fireplaces" into my browser. The very first hit sounded promising. It described, "an online shop with the biggest selection of fireplaces in Poland." I clicked on it and found brushes for fireplaces, pipes for fireplaces, wood for fireplaces and a dozen or so other fireplace-related categories but not a single fireplace. I couldn't believe my eyes, so I asked three of my friends to check whether I was missing something, but no. Not a single fireplace was to be found on that site. It felt like someone had opened a shop but neglected to fill the shelves with the most basic products.

In the Minimum Viable Product culture that is so prevalent in the digital world today, we can see tons of similar examples. Some banks don't provide ways to transfer money from one account to another. Shops empty your online shopping basket before you hit "buy". The lack of functionality doesn't allow you to initiate a purchase of a mobile phone plan or an insurance policy online and then complete it in the store (or the other way around). This list can go forever. Missing functionality (especially the crucial bits of it) often feels as if someone asked you to drink water from a sheet of paper. You might try but your chances of success are slim. Functionality is like the basic ingredients for cooking—without enough of it to complete a task there is no chance anyone will use your solution.

Reliability

Reliability means that you deliver on your promise and that you do it first time.[61] You carry out your service dependently and accurately. If you go to fix your car, you don't want to have to do it again two days later. Your trust in your mechanic would drop. In the same way, if your service is unreliable, your customers' trust in you will fall. But it gets even worse. If you have failed your customer once, their tolerance for further mistakes shrinks and they expect your service to be better next time around to compensate for the previous failure. Do you remember the "magic ratio" of positive versus negative events? Staying on the positive side of this ratio defines how reliable your brand is perceived to be. So, once you make a mistake that undermines your reliability, you need to deliver a few positive experiences to reestablish a positive emotional relationship with a disappointed customer. In other words, if you fail your customers, they will expect more from you, rather than less.

There is one more aspect critical to the perception of reliability, which I have already talked about, but I believe it is worth mentioning once more. If a customer contacts you with a problem that doesn't get resolved, their zone of tolerance shrinks rapidly. So, what is desired and what is adequate becomes the same. The good news is that a little positive surprise will be perceived as a great improvement. On the other hand, if the problem remains unresolved, their dissatisfaction will rapidly grow, leading them to deem your brand unreliable.

Usability

If you ever decide to send a package to Mexico you might find yourself in trouble. Somehow, the international delivery companies missed out on the fact that Mexican names are long and Mexican addresses are even longer. So, there is a high risk that once you enter the recipient details, they won't fit a standard form. It feels like a waste of time and it will most likely demotivate you from using this particular brand again. It is due to the lack of usability.

Over the last century usability and ergonomics have become a widely acknowledged quality of products and services. Usability is expressed by the ease of use and learnability. It determines that your goals are achieved efficiently and effectively.[62] It is the basis for how easy it is to book your tickets, choose an insurance policy or make a payment. It reinforces both functionality and reliability, and adds to them in the sense that it helps your customers meet their goals in an optimal manner. In 1998, Ben Schneiderman defined the basic principles of usability, which include:[63]

- usefulness, which basically means that a given solution should address the real needs of customers, and the provided functions should be relevant to their context;

- consistency, which indicates that you should use the commonly understood concepts, terms and metaphors, and present information in a natural and logical order;

- simplicity, which implies elimination of any unnecessary or irrelevant elements;

- communication, which means providing appropriate, clear, and timely feedback, putting related things together, and organising groups of actions with a beginning, middle, and end;

- error prevention and handling, which determines that your job is to prevent customers from making errors whenever possible as well as helping them to resolve those they run into;

- efficiency, which means that you need to help your customers to produce desired results without wasting their time, energy or materials.

These rules, although maybe not so fashionable today, are crucial to meeting the expectations of your customers and building a relationship with them. Yet, unintentionally, usability can be sacrificed amid the frenzy of adding new features and workflows. On the other hand, the optimisation efforts can lead to unnecessary oversimplification, taking control from the users and disempowering them. Years ago, Randy Pagulayan, who worked at Microsoft Game Studio, joked, "If a usability engineer designed a game, it would be most likely a single button announcing: 'To win, press here'."[64]

Aesthetics

Paul Hekkert, professor of form theory at Delft University of Technology, defines aesthetics as the pleasure (or displeasure) derived from the sensory-motor understanding of the world around us.[65,66] This understanding comes from the fact that people feel the quality of things or situations, and immediately know if they are to their liking.[67] Back in 2000, aesthetics was seen as the cherry on the top of a usable solution, but times have changed dramatically. We can blame Apple for this, I guess. Apple has shown the world that whatever solution is put on the market, it doesn't just need to work well, it also needs to look good. After the introduction of the iPhone, customers realised that they could demand products that are visually pleasing, and companies noticed that beauty sells.

Visual attractiveness is a foundation for building an emotional relationship between the customer and the product for two reasons. The first concerns the social aspect of our lives: we would rather surround ourselves with things that are beautiful than with things that are not. What is visually attractive (clothes, shoes, glasses, phones, cars, etc.) makes *us* more attractive. The second reason I have already mentioned in the previous chapter: when a product or a service looks good, we assume that it will also be more usable. Essentially, aesthetics is a way to convince our brains that we will need less energy for a given interaction, compared to one with a solution that is not visually pleasing. So, it is safe to say that although it sits with basics, aesthetics is an element that touches us on both pragmatic and affective levels. However, in the world today it is no longer an option to deliver products and services that are not aesthetically pleasing. In that sense we could say, paraphrasing Daniel Pink, that, "aesthetics has become democratised."[68]

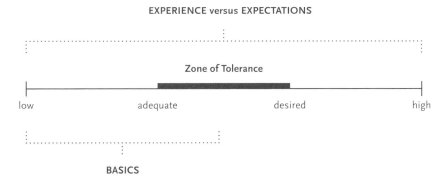

Satisfying pragmatic needs

Basics are crucial factors required for anyone to even consider signing up with your brand.★ If you look at the Zone of Tolerance you will find basics sitting between what is adequate to your customers and the space of competitive disadvantage, where your customers perceive your offering as below the acceptable level. This adequate level reflects the minimum of what you need to deliver on so that your customers don't start looking for alternatives. Basics are the foundation for our pragmatic reasoning, for satisfying the homo economicus in all of us.

It you drop the proverbial ball in this respect, your customers will become "reluctant customers", unwilling to either stay with you for much longer or to purchase more from your brand. It is because delivering on basics gives your customers a feeling of control over what is going on when they interact with your brand. It helps them experience competence and fulfilment, rather than incompetence and frustration.[69] But basics are not responsible for making them enjoy that interaction. It is the "motivators" that make your customers stay with your brand even though the straightforward value-for-money offer may no longer be the main attraction.

★   Back in 1984, Dr. Noriaki Kano, professor of Quality Management at To-kyo University of Science, proposed a model of product development and customer satisfaction widely known today as the Kano Model. The Basics described here reflect the threshold and the performance attributes in that model – a set of features that customers expect a product or service to have.

CHAPTER SIX
Motivators

Whatever we do in our lives (through interactions with other people, as well as products and services) either helps us or hinders us from "becoming the person we desire to be."[70] Certainly, many offerings make our lives more effective and efficient, but to catch our hearts, something more must be offered: something that connects to our values, something we would miss if it were gone, something that "makes our lives worth living."[71] In a way, every brand needs to become a means to making people feel happier about themselves if they want to trigger positive emotions and foster loyalty as a result. We will unpack the notion of happiness in the next chapter, but it's important to mention it here because the things we use are, in fact, a part of the autobiographical narrative constantly built and updated by our Remembering Self.[72] For any brand to be able to influence that narrative it needs to address at least one of the four motivators: empathy, fun, engagement or meaning. These are the aspects that must be met in order for you, to exceed the expectations of your customers and to trigger their emotional involvement with your brand.

Empathy

The most basic trigger that builds emotional engagement, and therefore loyalty, is empathy. Empathy is defined as, "caring, individualised attention provided to the customer."[73] Customers love brands that act like "partners", that care about them like a friend. I have previously mentioned the conundrum that customer service departments experience today. Their job used to be to offer

MOTIVATORS

affective value

Empathy   **Fun**   **Engagement**   **Meaning**

The Umami Threshold

Functionality   Reliability   Usability   Aesthetics

pragmatic value

BASICS

empathy.★ Yet, today, they are mostly about sales and protecting companies from their customers. Many companies might argue that they create personalised automatic service. But this is not the point. Customers want genuine, responsive and assuring support over time. They expect brands to make a sincere effort to understand and help them in a fair and caring way.

Zappos, an American online retailer, doesn't offer a unique product but it has managed to use empathy to stand out from the competition. If you want to chat with their customer service employee for hours or enquire about the best pizza place around, that's okay!★★ Zappos employees use empathy to build personal relationships with customers rather than just make a sale. Furthermore, the Zappos team is given freedom to do whatever they think is necessary to create a PEC (Personal Emotional Connection) with every customer. This often means they extend creative signs of appreciation, from waiving shipping fees to sending a bouquet of flowers. There are no scripts, just people on the other end of the line who are empowered to help you. This is why Zappos has probably one of the highest numbers of returning customers in the world.

Empathy can be demonstrated in a number of ways. For example, most people don't think about how their feet hit the ground when

★   Empathy is a great thing. But, as Paul Bloom, a Canadian American psychologist and the Brooks and Suzanne Ragen Professor of Psychology and Cognitive Science at Yale University, argues, sometimes it can also make us biased towards people who are similar to us, who are closer rather than far away. It is enumerated: we feel empathy towards one person but not towards many, so in a way we are more concerned about a child who just fell from a tree than we are about climate change. Finally, it is crucial to understand that empathy can be politically weaponised. It can be used to evoke and direct our emotions in ways that can be harmful to us, to others and also to the planet itself.[74]

★★   The record for the longest call at Zappos call centre is a whooping 10 hours, 51 minutes, during which the consultant took only one break.

they run, not realising that the arch support of their shoe, the length of their foot, and the surfaces they typically run on, play an important role in their health. So, before you buy a pair of running shoes at some Nike stores, the employees will ask you to get on a treadmill and they will measure your stride so they can recommend the shoes that best meet your needs. Such stories build a feeling in customers that they are seen as valuable, and therefore their emotional relationship with your brand strengthens.

Empathy proves to be the most powerful tool when things go wrong (and it is safe to assume that some of your customers will get annoyed by you at some point in time). Any such situation runs the risk of creating a story that sheds a negative light on your brand. In defence, many companies try to blame the customer for whatever has gone wrong. They may say that the customer didn't understand the agreement, that they carried out the procedure incorrectly, that they could have acted sooner. You might be surprised to know that whenever a customer reaches out to a provider, they are 90 percent sure they will be blamed for the situation. How is such blame perceived? An already annoyed customer gets annoyed for the second time – they are not only unhappy with whatever went wrong with the service, they also feel they are now being called a liar or at least a sloppy creature. The already negative story forming in their mind gets reinforced. The defensive posture of so many brands pushes their customers to become active detractors.

These companies don't realise the power of an honest and authentic "I'm sorry" strategy, which is the most important step whenever you want to build your competitive advantage based on empathy. If you apologise for whatever happened (regardless of whether it was your company's fault or the customer's fault) you will most likely create a positive surprise and build a foundation for the customer to engage in further interaction with an open mind. The initial level of negativity will be lowered, and even if you are unable to resolve a given problem to the advantage of your customer, they will most likely be willing to give you a second chance.

Fun

"Things are fun when they attract, capture, and hold our attention by provoking new or unusual perceptions, arousing emotions in contexts that typically arouse none, or arousing emotions not typically aroused in a given context."[75] We often experience fun during entertainment, recreation, or sports. Fun is also experienced during mental challenges such as solving problems, playing music, and discovering something new. In gentler forms it can be about laughing at late-night comedy shows, listening to music, watching movies or simply relaxing. But above all, fun is about adding an element of surprise and joy that could not be predicted. There is one thing worth mentioning: fun requires an adequate level of complexity, otherwise it won't be either sufficiently surprising or sufficiently engaging.[76]

For example, in 2012, Anthon Berg, a Danish chocolate manufacturer, decided to open an unusual pop-up store. This was in response to the dreary results of a poll run with Danes which showed that only two percent of Danish men were willing to celebrate Valentine's Day, while the vast majority had written it off as a meaningless holiday.[77] So, the company invited a well-known neuroscientist, Paul Zak from the Claremont Graduate University (also known as Dr Love), to make a "scientific love experiment" based on the observation that levels of oxytocin in the blood of men increase by 27.5 percent after they vocalise love for their partners.[78] Based on this observation, the pop-up store offered boxes of candy that were marked with surprising price tags: *Don't comment on your significant other's driving for a week* or *Serve breakfast in bed*. The payment was conducted in the form of a Facebook pledge to a friend to carry out a specific act of kindness. The most popular promise turned out to be: *Help clean a friend's house.*★ The concept proved to be so popular that people were willing to queue for over an hour to get their box of chocolates and commit to their pledge. The cool outcome was that almost everyone kept their promise.

★   Hardly anyone touched the box labelled: *A week where you don't lie to your father.*

Having fun is about experiencing immediate pleasure from an interaction and this can be a tool for evoking positive emotions such as delight, surprise, enjoyment or gratification. Ben Schneiderman wrote, "Fun-filled experiences are playful and liberating — they make you smile. They are a break from the ordinary and bring satisfying feelings of pleasure for body and mind."[79] Fun makes your offering more relatable and it triggers an emotional connection with your brand. In that sense, both empathy and fun address the needs of our Experiencing Selves. They make the moments we live though enjoyable and therefore memorable. They are a great way to trigger positive surprise and make our brain feel at ease, and therefore open to exploration of whatever else your brand might have to offer.

Engagement

Engagement is a psychological state where we are deeply immersed in an activity (like, for example, writing a book).[80] It lasts over time and keeps us focused. It is a sense of togetherness that we as customers want to experience. Engagement is a positive, fulfilling state of mind that is characterised by vigour, dedication, and absorption.[81] Above all, engagement is something that we enjoy intrinsically because it satisfies "the inherent tendency to seek out novelty and challenges, to exercise one's capacities, to explore and to learn."[82],★

Engaging experiences help connect people with what really matters to them. You can create such connections by supporting people's needs for learning and growth, and for belonging.[83] Gallup research shows that, in retail banking, customers who are fully engaged bring

---

★   It is important to recognise that engagement is different from motivation. Motivation is getting us to do something. Engagement is doing it. It is a genuine flow while progressing with an activity and the willingness to re-engage without being pushed and pressed to do so. Medium is a great example. It is designed in a way that truly supports the act of writing and has a number of stimuli that make many of us return here of our own accord without being pestered to do so.

37 percent more annual revenue to their primary bank, compared with customers who are actively disengaged.[84] Fully engaged banking customers also have more products with their bank, from checking and savings accounts to mortgages and loans. But what is often seen as engagement—commenting, clicking or sharing on social media—is, in fact, an illusion.[85] When you want to engage your customers, you want to motivate them to consciously use what your brand offers over time, to build an intentional and meaningful interaction with you.

My favourite example of building such engagement is Umpqua Bank. They see themselves as catalysts for local community building and so they offer their branches (called "stores") as spaces for organising events like theatre performances or poetry readings. These stores feature conference rooms for anyone in the community to use free of charge, art installations that reflect the local culture, and coffee bars. They further build engagement on the community level through their banking services. For example, they offer better credit for the local businesses that collaborate together. In this way, Umpqua creates highly engaged customers, who are willing to make their brand work for them and are open to trying new offerings and services. This behaviour confirms Gallup's analysis, which has found that fully engaged customers are more loyal and profitable than average customers, both in good economic times and in bad.

Meaning

TOMS began in 2006 when its founder, Blake Mycoskie, travelled to Argentina and saw countless children walking around barefoot. It inspired him to start a business with the One for One model in mind. He decided that, for every pair of shoes the company sold, they would give a pair to a child. After selling the first 10 000 pairs, Mycoskie, his family, and a few others travelled to Argentina to do their first shoe drop. Years later, the company has given away thousands of shoes throughout the world. The TOMS brand began as a company, but it has become a story and a worldwide initiative looking for ways to give back and in that way to offer meaning to a purchase of shoes.[86] TOMS is one of the brands that addresses the human need for meaning, which is well captured in the words of professor Martin Seligman as, "belonging to and serving something that you believe is bigger than the self."[87]

There are a number of views of what brings meaning to people. For example, Nathan Shedroff, co-author of *Making Meaning,* proposes that meaning is created by addressing a set of core values that depict ways in which people interact with others and the world in the deepest way.[88,★] On the other hand, Amy Bucher, author of *Engaged,* argues that meaning is derived from the choices we make.[89] People make choices that make them feel competent and autonomous rather than constrained and overwhelmed. There is one more perspective on meaning in experiences I would like to bring forward. J. Robert Rossman and Mathew D. Deurden, authors of *Designing Experiences,* write that, "meaningful experiences teach us something about ourselves and expand our knowledge about the world."[90] They see discovery as a key element of meaning-making that helps us figure out our personality and our worldview, that offers us new insights and gives us the opportunity of learning. These three perspectives certainly are key elements of meaning in the context of designing an experience, but there is one core aspect that binds them.

Viktor Frankl famously wrote that: "Man's main concern is not to gain pleasure or to avoid pain but rather to see a meaning in his life. [...] People have enough to live, but nothing to live for; they have the means but no meaning."[91] We are constantly in pursuit of meaning in our existence, whether consciously or subconsciously. People want to do meaningful work, experience meaningful leisure activities, attain more impact. This need is an expression of what Aristotle called *eudaemonia* (translated as "flourishing"). There are a few aspects that are crucial to Aristotle's definition. Firstly, he argued that flourishing is a process, not a state.[92] Then, he stated that it is a matter of how

★   These core values include: Accomplishment, Beauty, Creation, Community, Duty, Enlightenment, Freedom, Harmony, Justice, Oneness, Redemption, Security, Truth, Validation and Wonder.

well we live our lives, whatever the circumstances. Finally, Aristotle argued that people can only flourish through interactions with others and with the world that bring greater value than that of achieving a direct goal. Taking an Aristotelian perspective on meaning signifies that meaning:

- is an ultimate goal;
- this goal needs to match personal values;
- it needs to reflect the rational and the emotional side of humans;
- it advances a greater common good that is aligned with individual happiness.

Brands can help us begin to fulfil this need. Look at Tesla. Many people choosing their car do so in search for meaning: be it a less negative impact on the environment or the support of the Mars mission. Those who choose products by the Body Shop, Smashbox or Kevin Murphy's often do so to protect animals from being abused as test subjects. The positive psychology professor, Martin Seligman, summarised this ultimate search for meaning as, "knowing what your higher strengths are and deploying them in the service of something larger than you are."[93] So, in fact, you won't be designing meaning. You will be designing for your customers to find their own meaning that resonates with them, and that helps them create value that goes beyond their own needs.

Tapping into latent needs

As I mentioned earlier, we all strive to become better versions of our-selves. By addressing the motivators, the brands we use enable us to do this. Empathy makes us feel listened to, so it builds on related-ness, fun addresses our need for instant gratification and enjoyment, engagement provides us with flow, and meaning gives us a sense that what we do extends beyond ourselves. Addressing these latent needs not only satisfies the moment-to-moment desires of the Experiencing Self, but prompts our Remembering Self to store memories that become the narratives we live by. As we live the lives we would like to live, we feel happier, and in order to feel happier, we engage with the brands that help us to do so.

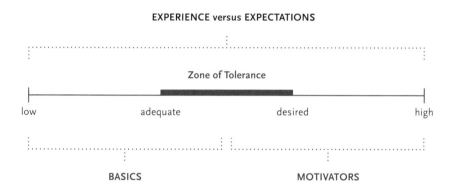

EXPERIENCE versus EXPECTATIONS

Zone of Tolerance

low   adequate   desired   high

BASICS   MOTIVATORS

CHAPTER SEVEN
The Umami of Business

Building remarkable experiences for your customers is a work of balance that requires considering both basics and motivators when doing so. It is due to the fact that customer satisfaction and dis-satisfaction is not a continuum, with one increasing as the other diminishes.★ If you work on addressing basics, customers' dissatis-faction may, indeed, decrease but this doesn't mean that their satis-faction will automatically grow. In addition, whenever you attempt to increase motivators but neglect basics, you would be mistaken in assuming that overall customer satisfaction will rise. Only if you address both motivators and basics will customers begin to engage with you on the emotional level. If you just work on basics but neglect motivators, there will be few complaints but also little motivation for connecting with your brand. Your service will be viewed as value for money and you will build a purely transactional relationship with your customers.

On the other hand, if you address motivators but neglect basics, you will find yourself in a situation where your offering will be seen as exciting but its quality not up to scratch. Your customers will be motivated to try it but they will be quickly disappointed and their Zone of Tolerance will narrow. Over time, they may abandon you for another brand that fulfils their pragmatic needs, even if they do so with a heavy heart. Finally, if you neglect both motivators and basics,

★ "The factors that lead to satisfaction (achievement, intrinsic interest in the work, responsibility, and advancement) are mostly unipolar; that is, they contribute very little to job dissatisfaction. Conversely, the dis-satisfiers (company policy and administrative practices, supervision, interpersonal relationships, working conditions, and salary) contribute very little to job satisfaction."

MOTIVATORS

affective value

Empathy   **Fun**   **Engagement**   **Meaning**

The Umami Threshold

Functionality   **Reliability**   **Usability**   **Aesthetics**

pragmatic value

BASICS

your customers will not be motivated by your offering and will have many complaints. They may stay with you because they are bound by a contract of sorts but they will remain passive and conservative in their choices, and will leave as soon as possible while constantly bad-mouthing you.

Negativity bias

There is one thing worth remembering when it comes to basics: customers have an easier time talking about these, compared to talking about motivators.★ This is an expression of negativity bias. Negative bias is our tendency to not only register negative events more readily but also to dwell on them more. Also known as "positive — negative asymmetry", this bias means that negative events have a greater impact on our brains than positive ones, which directly relates to our survival instinct. I have already talked about how our brain reacts to dopamine and adrenaline but let me outline it once more. If your brand addresses the basics, a small amount of dopamine is released into your customers' bloodstream so they are willing to use what your brand offers them. If the basics are neglected, their experience drops below adequate and customers get a powerful shot of adrenaline, which invokes in them a feeling of danger. They may not be able to move away from your brand right away but they will do their best to minimise further exposure to the unpleasantness they have experienced.[94] So, if you fall short on basics, your customers will not only become passive and conservative users of your offering but they will also easily recall your shortcomings, as these shortcomings trigger their survival instinct.

Moreover, we humans are less motivated by the idea of gaining something than we are by avoiding a loss. So, if your offering misses any of the basics, your customers will get the impression that they are wasting time, money or attention and therefore they are inclined to a stronger reaction to it, followed by an easier recall of that fact

★   They are also more inclined to say more about the negative aspects of your offering than about the positive ones.

afterward. If, on the other hand, you deliver on the motivators, customers have a feeling of reward, which is a less strong motivator for action and recall.

Finally, negative comments are more likely to be perceived as a valid assessment for the overall performance of your brand, as negative information is seen as having greater validity compared to positive information. So if you don't deliver on basics, your customers will be quick to judge you as unreliable and you won't stop hearing about it, which is a trap of its own. Since you hear more about basics than about motivators, it is only natural to focus on these and try to fix them. This is the negative bias playing a trick on you — the negative feedback makes you focus on forever fixing basics rather than expanding on your motivators. Yet, every problem you resolve will generate another set of problems, and therefore you will be fixing the basics forever. And you don't want to just solve a problem to stand out in the market. You want to motivate your customers to see your brand as an enabler for their happiness.

Talking about emotions

Apart from the fact that our reactions are hard-wired to favour negativity, we humans are also not good at talking about motivators, as motivators are linked to emotions and expressing emotions is not an easy task.[95] So, customers are more likely to talk about the "concrete" pragmatic (likely negative) elements of your offering, than about the "fuzzy" emotional stuff. This is due to the fact that emotions are born from the perception of visceral reactions in our body rather than through our consciousness and, unfortunately, this information is not very precise.[96]

Our knowledge about our emotional state is not only contextualised by our sensory, motor, and somato-visceral reactions but also driven by our ability to express emotions.[97] People who are low in emotional granularity report their experiences using labels such as "angry," "happy," and so on, to represent only the general aspects of their internal state (typically pleasure or displeasure).

Lisa Feldman Barrett explains such low granularity in perceiving emotions through the response of one of her students to the events of September 11, 2001, "I felt a bunch of things I couldn't put my finger on. Maybe anger, confusion, fear. I just felt bad on September 11, really bad." More generally, individuals with low emotional granularity use emotion-related words such as "happy" and "excited" to mean "pleasant," and the terms "sad" and "angry" to mean "unpleasant." Their ability to express emotions more precisely is very limited.

On the other hand, people higher in emotional granularity report their experiences in more subtle terms. For example, another student cited by Professor Barrett who was higher in emotional granularity, said, "My first reaction was terrible sadness. But the second reaction was that of anger, because you can't do anything with the sadness." This student was communicating fairly distinct experiences and distinguishing them by the degree of reaction they seemed to induce.[98] So, it is crucial to remember that many of your customers may have trouble naming their emotions towards your brand and, therefore, they will be more inclined to avoid talking about emotions (which are primarily related to motivators) in the first place, and, instead, focus on the aspects of your offering that fire their negativity bias (which are primarily related to basics).

A happier version of you

Let's look at basics and motivators from one more angle. Basics are an expression of a problem-driven approach to your offering. Fixing basics is an activity focused on removing problems (like making something more usable, cheaper or safer). It is motivated by reducing a discrepancy between how things are done today and how they could be seemingly done in the future. In a way, when addressing basics, your goal is to "keep the demons asleep"; to neutralise, resolve or avoid situations that invoke negative emotions.[99]

However, addressing the negative aspects of your offering doesn't necessarily mean that the experience will be positive. In a way, curing a problem allows you to move from the negative to the neutral state, but the transition from the neutral to the positive state requires more than just resolving problems. There is a great difference between having a functional banking service and a feeling of financial security for yourself and your family. It is about making your customers feel empowered when they interact with your brand.

Motivators are your means to go beyond the problem-solving approach to your offering. They first and foremost trigger a positive emotional response.[100] They offer an appearance of authenticity and ingenuity.[101] They induce joy and they offer meaning. They are the factors that offer your customers a feeling of fulfilment and make them feel like they live a good and happy life. And as I mentioned before, they give people the opportunity to become the better versions of themselves based on these simple rules: pleasure is better than pain; intense absorption is better than lethargic emptiness; relatedness to others is better than loneliness or hostility.

To be happy is a quality in itself. Happiness is a major, if not the ultimate, goal for every human.[102] If asked to make three wishes for "anything at all", Sheri Broyles, a professor for the Mayborn School of Journalism, found happiness to be the most common wish people have.[103] Sonja Lyubomirsky wrote that happiness consists of two components: the experience of joy, contentment and positive emotion combined with a sense that your life is good, meaningful and worthwhile.[104] Happy people are healthier, more successful and contribute more to the lives of others.[105] They are also more open to try and use the different offerings your brand offers them.

Brands and their offerings can contribute to increasing this happiness through addressing the motivators, which, if you think about it, are expressions of an ideal future state (rather than the undesirable current state that is depicted through basics). So, if you sit down to design your next offering, you might think about it from the perspective of a great product or a great service. This would be a very traditional approach. You might also see your offering as a tool for enjoying a certain activity, like, for example, having a mobile application to manage your finances or exercising on a bicycle. But there is one more perspective you might consider. You could think of how your offering is going to make people feel about themselves;[106] whether it gives them the power to see themselves as autonomous, competent and connected.[107] Once you achieve that, you can be sure the Remembering Self of your customers will be happy to regard your offering as something to keep on using and keep talking about. This is the way to create an emotional bond with your customers rather than just a transactional one.[108]

"Alice: Would you tell me, please,
which way I ought to go from here?

The Cheshire Cat: That depends
a good deal on where you want to get to.

Alice: I don't much care where.

The Cheshire Cat: Then it doesn't much matter
which way you go.

Alice: ...So long as I get somewhere.

The Cheshire Cat: Oh, you're sure to do that,
if only you walk long enough."

Lewis Carroll
Alice in Wonderland

PART II

Defining Your Umami Strategy

CHAPTER ONE

The Danger of Playing It Safe

For five years now, almost every Wednesday, I have been going to the local market to shop at Mr Herb's stall. Who is Mr Herb? Years ago, he went with his family on holiday to Italy and became enchanted with their local markets. He asked himself, "Why can't we have that in Poland?" Upon returning home, he decided to start an eco-farm and today, he is a major supplier to the best local restaurants, including some holding Michelin stars. In addition, twice a week, he sells his amazing vegetables to regular folk like myself. This might sound like a regular enough story but there is more to it.

In most markets, you are offered produce selected by the seller. With Mr Herb you choose it yourself. You can smell every tomato, touch every beetroot and try out every green leaf before you purchase it. You can take all the time in the world to make your selection and what a pleasure it is not to be rushed because another customer is waiting in line. When it comes to paying, there is some weighing and some calculating involved. But the result seems to be strangely consistent: if we have the IKEA bag half-filled we pay about 10 euros. If it is filled to the brim, we pay 25 euros. Frankly, I sometimes think that this process of summing up is a bit of theatre—they know what they are going to charge you once you get your bag in front of them. And every time I shop there, I have this feeling of getting an amazing bargain, often topped with a gift.

Some weeks ago, I bumped into Mr Herb himself. He was worried that some of his tomatoes were not fresh enough.

"It will destroy my reputation", he said.

"It's not going to be that easy", was my reply, "One rotten tomato is not going to destroy the value of this amazing experience. Your customers just love shopping with you, Sir."

What makes Mr Herb so unique? What makes me tell stories about him to anyone who cares to listen (yourself included) when I rarely do so about other brands, products and services?

Offering just a little bit

Many companies, when trying to attract customers, aim to offer solutions that are "just a little bit better" than what the competition provides. If your competitor makes a new application, you will improve yours. If they add a new feature or a new offer, you will try to do the same, and make it just a little more attractive. Unfortunately, nobody is excited by the same but a little better. In his book *Purple Cow*, Seth Godin says, "offering a little bit is a waste of time. The people are open to hearing your story only if it's truly remarkable: otherwise you're invisible."[109] Yet, so many brands go for those little improvements anyway. Why? Most companies aim to satisfy the average customer, someone who is not keen on risk and who wants to use solutions that feel familiar. It may seem like a smart approach on the face of it, but it is not. Familiar things are what your customers expect, so their Remembering Selves are not likely to remember such an offering and therefore, your brand.

There are two large discount grocery stores in our neighbourhood. For years, neither shop provided hand-held shopping baskets. You could either take a large trolley or carry the products in your hands. In many ways this made sense, as about 85 percent of customers shopped on Saturdays and were buying stuff for the entire week for the whole family. But these customers were looking for bargains. They were purchasing a lot but not the products that had the highest mark-up and were most profitable for the company.

It took some years for both chains to realise that the people who were coming there three times a week and buying five products were those spending significantly more money than the "regular" customers. And both chains were effectively discouraging them from doing so by not offering hand-held baskets. While focusing on the behaviour of the majority, they were ignoring the fact that these customers were the critical minority for them: people who wanted to buy a 14-euro bottle of wine, rather than one that cost four euros. These were people who could make shopping at a discount stores fashionable.

Finally, one brand got the point and introduced small shopping baskets, a reasonable selection of wine and other upmarket products. By doing so, it altered grocery shopping behaviour across the country. Suddenly, it was no longer considered embarrassing to shop at a discount store. It was smart thinking. Catering for the majority of customers would never have changed that situation. The majority were not interested in buying expensive cheese and wine. They were not looking for bio-bananas and hummus. But once these products were introduced into the store, once the fashionable people kept on purchasing them, the more conservative customers got ready to try them too. It was the innovation adaptation curve in the making (also called "Moore's diffusion curve").★ Through this model, Geoff Moore outlined

★   Moore's idea diffusion curve represents how a successful business innovation moves, from left to right, and affects more customers until it finally reaches the entire population. On the x-axis you can see the different groups the idea affects over time. The y-axis shows how many people belong to each group.

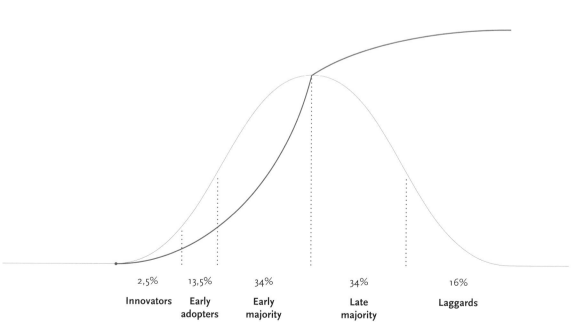

| 2,5% | 13,5% | 34% | 34% | 16% |
| Innovators | Early adopters | Early majority | Late majority | Laggards |

how ideas and products spread across a population of customers, from innovators and early adopters, to early and late majority, through to laggards. While Moore predominantly focused on spread of technology, his insight applies to any offering, any product and any brand.

Here lies a challenge though. While the market share grows most when your offering is adopted by the biggest volume of customers (early and late majority), the value of your brand is tightly connected to the level of influence stemming from innovators and early adopters. In other words, your early adopters are your tool to convince the rest of the curve about the worth of your offering.[110] Joe Pine and Jim Gilmore call it the "battle for customer attention, time and money."[111] This happens because those customers jaded with the unlimited choice of today's market refuse to pay attention to yet another offering that is almost the same.

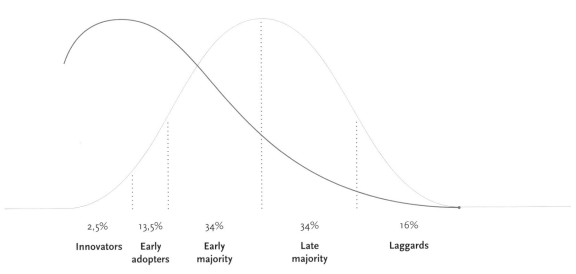

2,5%	13,5%	34%	34%	16%
Innovators	Early adopters	Early majority	Late majority	Laggards

Yet, whenever a company attempts to create something entirely new, it makes their decision-makers uncomfortable. How can they know it will be a success? The thing is, there are no guarantees. One thing is certain, though. If you choose to stay safe, there is little risk that people will criticise your solution. If you choose to be different it is likely that some customers (especially the more conservative ones) might dislike your proposition. This initial dislike feels too risky for many companies. It is, indeed, safer to offer an incremental change (like an extra discount or a slightly better offer) than to try to go "head first" with a new idea. Look at the brands around you. Do they really differ from each other? Not much. What you see is not differentiation but imitation. It seems like every brand is running as fast as they can to... stand still. So, here's the painful truth: no matter what business you are in, you are most likely surrounded by competition. Doing what others are doing is not going to help you. You need a new way of thinking. A new approach.

Heterogeneously homogeneous

Let's face it: abundance has lost its status. Everybody is used to having an unlimited selection, whether it comes to jams, holiday offerings or insurances. Your next bag of almost-the-same-as-the-last-one-but-new-and-improved chips is not going to make much difference. The only thing you might provoke is a terror of choice. While having no choice is almost unbearable for people, having too much choice is even worse. In his book, *The Paradox of Choice*, professor of social theory and action at Swarthmore College, Barry Schwartz, says, "Learning to choose is hard. Learning to choose well is harder. And learning to choose well in a world of unlimited possibilities is harder still, perhaps too hard."[112] So, what do people do if they face unlimited choice? They often choose not to choose at all.

There is another trap of doing more of the same: the next solution you offer your customers is increasingly trivial. If you are a bank, you might offer 2.1 percent on your customers' savings, rather than two percent, like your competition. One of my clients in the finance industry noticed that such actions lead to the formation of a new

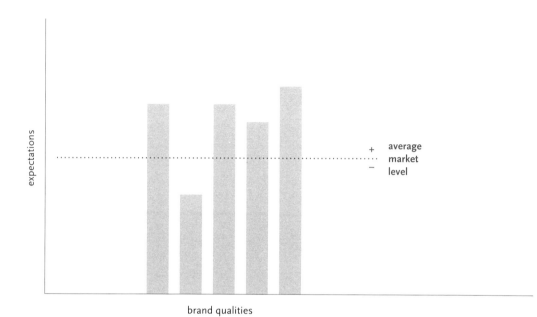

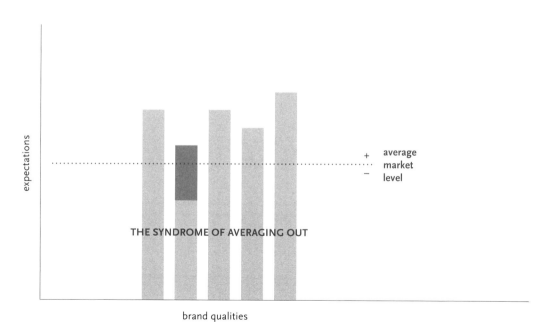

THE SYNDROME OF AVERAGING OUT

customer behaviour they call "tornadoing". About 35 percent of customers who opened an account, triggered by a new offer, tended to keep their savings there for as long as the offer was running, but once the promotion was over, transferred their money back to their old account. In the short term, it might look as though the promotion has worked, but has it? I don't think any business is looking for such tornado behaviour.

The last pitfall regards placing focus on improving your weaknesses compared to the competition, rather than looking for a meaningful differentiator. In her book, *Different: Escaping the Competitive Herd*, Professor Young Moon talks about this phenomenon.[113] When she first started teaching, she came up with the idea of providing mid-term feedback to her students. After a few weeks, it became apparent that this feedback led to everybody improving on their weaknesses rather than building on their strengths. The creative students focused on working on their analytical skills, and the analytical students tried to be more creative, which eventually led to the discussion in the classroom losing its edge.

The same thing happens to brands. As soon as you start comparing yourself to others, you focus on eliminating the differences rather than accentuating them. You tend to solely concentrate on fixing the "vulnerabilities" of your brand (your basics) in favour of improving on your strengths (your motivators). This primal herd-like behaviour makes you want to keep your competition not too close but not too far away either. This is why companies like McDonalds serve coffee and companies like Starbucks offer warm snacks. This well-intended effort to monitor your competitive position and to improve in relation to it leads to the syndrome of averaging out. Every brand on the market is different but at the same time almost the same. Yet, as Professor Moon notices, "the true differentiation—sustainable differentiation—is rarely a function of well-roundedness; it is typically a function of lopsidedness."

I can almost see the doubt in your eyes as you read this. What about the rankings? What about the benchmarking measures? You need to understand that they can become a trap for your creativity.

John Kotter, leadership professor at Harvard Business School, explains that "benchmarking is done in an attempt to capture best practices on the market—behaviours, methods or systems which some sort of research shows the very top firms (those with the best scores based on some assessment) use to gain and hold that top position."[114] The problem is that these best practices either work in specific set-ups or become outdated over time (which is probably even more dangerous). They represent an arbitrary "industry standard", which is one of the reasons why the market averaging syndrome is so strong. Because if you want to differentiate, you are not going to fit into any standard that was defined based on past practices. You are pioneering a new standard, a new way of doing things.

Meaningfully different

Remember the troubles of Boeing? When Bill Allen was the CEO (1945–1968), the company was "eating, breathing, and sleeping the world of aeronautics."[115] During that time, Boeing developed the 737 model, the most successful aircraft of its time. By 1990, the company was the unquestioned number one in the business of civil aviation. This was not for the love of money but for the love of planes and flying. What Allen understood was that "meeting the technological challenges of supreme magnitude" was a way to build a company that was truly remarkable, that was challenging its market by being outstanding. This approach resulted in Boeing facing no real competition in that period.

Thirty years later, the new CEO, Phil Condit, announced that Boeing would now deliver a "value based environment where unit cost, return on investment, shareholder return are the measures by which [everything] will be judged."[116] This very decision led to Boeing facing an unimaginable situation a few years later. American Airlines, their long-standing customer, chose to buy their jets from Airbus. To win the contract back, Boeing quit developing the new plane they were working on. Instead, they decided to upgrade their 737 machine. It is worth mentioning that Boeing had already updated that model in 1984, again in 1997, and once more in 2017.

However, the low frame of the 737, which used to be ideal for loading and unloading cargo, limited the size of the engine it could fit. To make the engine larger, the engineers had to move it forward. This caused the plane's nose to tip upwards, which sometimes caused the plane to stall. To get around this, they developed an automated anti-stall system (MCAS) to point the nose downwards whenever a plane risked stalling. This was just one of many workarounds the engineers had to work through. The *New York Times* revealed that:[117]

> "Inside Boeing, the race was on. Roughly six months after the project's launch, engineers were already documenting the differences between the Max and its predecessor, meaning they already had preliminary designs for the Max — a fast turnaround, according to an engineer who worked on the project. 'The timeline was extremely compressed,' he said. 'It was go, go, go.'
>
> One former designer on the team working on flight controls for the Max said the group had at times produced 16 technical drawings a week, double the normal rate, 'They basically said, 'We need something now.'
>
> A technician who assembles wiring on the Max said that in the first months of development, rushed designers were delivering sloppy blueprints to him. He was told that the instructions for the wiring would be cleaned up later in the process. His internal assembly designs for the Max, he said, still include omissions today, like not specifying which tools to use to install a certain wire, a situation that could lead to a faulty connection."

Boeing executives kept repeating, "We aim to offer the best value to customers, including operating economics as well as timing, which was clearly a strong factor. Safety is our highest priority as we design, build and support our airplanes." But it looks as though, in that race with time, far too many corners were cut, which led to grounding 737 Max aircrafts in March 2019, after two plane crashes within five months, which caused the deaths of 648 passengers.

What Bill Allen understood (and Phil Condit didn't) was that in order to lead the market, you need to bet on the few things that you want to turn into your differentiators (like, for example, technological excellence) and then you have to mercilessly build on them.[118] This is exactly the conclusion I came to when thinking about Mr Herb and his approach to business. Is he losing money on his rather rough calculation of what his customers purchase? I am sure he is. Is he left with the worst produce at the end of the day after everybody has selected the juiciest tomatoes and cucumbers? Certainly. But he also works with the best restaurateurs and is celebrated across culinary circles. Articles are written about him. He has thousands of followers on Facebook and Instagram. He is sought after.

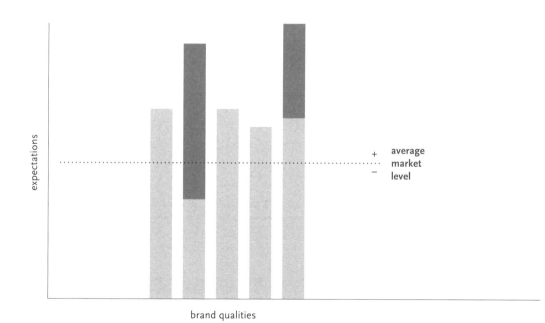

Yes, daring is risky. But at the end of the day it is the only thing that truly pays off. My hope is that the Umami Approach will support you in becoming different through these four steps:

- setting an Umami Baseline created out of the word of mouth your customers share about your brand;

- defining your aspirational Umami Vision;

- choosing your Edges — the differentiators that make your experience stand out, and;

- formulating powerful and actionable Umami Metrics that will become your prioritisation tool.

Together, these aim to help you create your unique experiential blend, which will inform the stories your customers share and make you stand out in the overcrowded market.

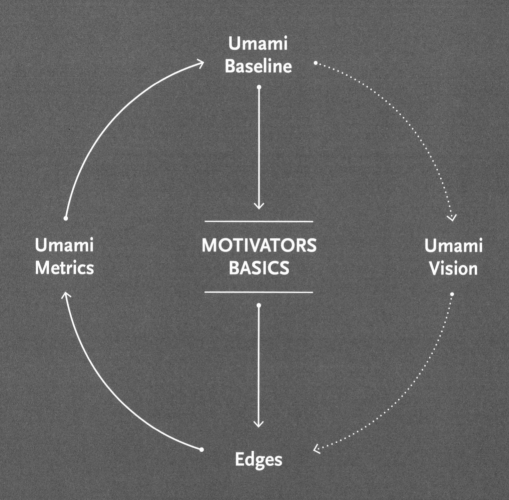

Umami
Baseline

MOTIVATORS
BASICS

Umami
Metrics

Umami
Vision

Edges

CHAPTER TWO

The Umami Baseline

Have you ever divorced a company? Decided that you no longer want
to be associated with a particular brand? We all naturally relate to
brands in a similar way that we relate to people.[119] Just as our relationships with people rise and fall, so do our relationships with brands.
But how do we get to understand which brand to choose and which
not? The official name for the stories that make or break deals with
brands is "word of mouth". In a way, word of mouth stories are our
instruments in the search for meaning in respect to our relationships
with brands, products and services.[120] And once customers create
a story about a brand, product or service, they are inclined to share
it with others.

The nature of word of mouth

The impact of word of mouth had already been investigated as early as
the 1950s. In a *Fortune* article, William Whyte Jr, an American urban-
ist, organisational analyst and journalist, demonstrated the importance of word of mouth as a fundamental influence on consumer
choice in the marketplace by showing how information about new
air-conditioners, TV sets and even doctors spread across American
neighbourhoods.[121] He was able to directly relate it to the web of
neighbourly connections (yeah, the internet had a slightly more physical incarnation in those days) proving that people shared stories about
their purchases and their favourable comments aided acceptance
of new products, while unfavourable comments hindered it. This
observation led to coining a proverb: "your best salesman is a satisfied customer."[122]

Research has also shown that word of mouth takes the shape of
the letter 'U'.[123] Very positive and very negative stories are repeated

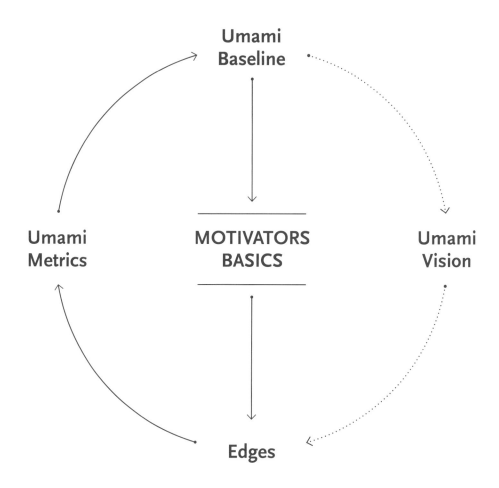

Umami
Baseline

MOTIVATORS
BASICS

Umami
Vision

Umami
Metrics

Edges

much more often than those that are just slightly positive or slightly negative (this is related to what our Remembering Self remembers). Here is a catch though: we overreact to the bad stories while under-reacting to the good ones and, consequently, we share the negative stories more often than the positive ones.

Back in 2015, we conducted a large study regarding the effects of word of mouth on the business of a Polish telecom company, Play. (I will go into further depth about this study later, but I would like to bring forward one result now.) We asked 1000 customers to write down the stories they shared with others about that brand. At the end we asked who they shared these stories with and how often. It turned out that, on average, positive stories were told to about six people (mostly family and close friends) while negative stories were shared with 11 people on average (and these included anyone who would listen — remote acquaintances and even strangers). We also found that, while the positive story lost its freshness after a year or two, the negative ones were being repeated even after seven years.

It is impossible to understand people's intentions while ignoring the stories they tell.[124] People love to share stories about the brands they use. We tell our friends about great holiday destinations, chat with our neighbours about good deals and discuss with our coworkers changes in management. We tweet, write reviews and gossip on social media. This leads to over a hundred million conversations about brands per hour.[125] In fact, word of mouth is the primary factor behind up to 50 percent of purchasing decisions made today. For example, one word of mouth conversation can lead to up to a 200 euro increase in restaurant sales. A book with a good number of five-star reviews on Amazon is more likely to sell 20 more books than one that doesn't have those. Word of mouth is said to have three times more impact on purchasing decisions than advertising today (and think of how expensive advertising is). It leads some brands and their offerings to catch on, and some to fail. It is so effective for two reasons. You know that advertising will only tell you about how great a given brand and its offering is. Word of mouth is much more persuasive. You know you will get not only the promise, but you will hear the nitty gritty details of how things truly work. Word of mouth is also much more targeted. Advertising targets a large variety of customers, so naturally it is kept at a high level of abstraction. Your friends will provide you with the information that is relevant to you.[126]

Capturing word of mouth

Since the power of word of mouth has been proven over and over again for the last 70 years, it is only natural that companies pay quite a bit of attention to it. They collect the stories customers tell about them via different market research tools that crawl the web and social media looking for any mention of the name of their products and services. What companies don't realise is that only about seven per-cent of word of mouth happens online.[127] People are often surprised to hear that. It seems like the number is far too low. But if you think about it — most of your interactions about different brands take place offline, with your family, friends and colleagues. Furthermore, the sto-ries told offline are much more convincing than those you encounter online for two reasons: you hear them from the mouth of a person you know, and you have the ability to ask for more details. Unfortunately, this word of mouth is almost never captured by traditional market research methods.

Before we continue, I would like to make one point here. The bot-tom line of any customer research is twofold. One thing you most likely want is to detect that failure as soon as possible, in order to immediately recover from it. The other thing you most likely would want is to detect as early as possible an upcoming opportunity that you might exploit to your advantage. In other words, you hope to spot an upcoming change before your competitors do, while you hope to avoid the so-called "Kodak moment", a situation where you are so invested in the current business that you are not able to see the shift in the market that might in time render you irrelevant.

I am sure you do this by running market research studies. However, as much as the traditional market research offers you breadth of insight, it does not necessarily go into the depth of it. You look at data that has been aggregated and averaged for you. It has information about the general perception, but it misses out the actual variability of the data. So, you see what the majority of people think but you miss out on finding people who think differently. And these people might be your early detectors of change or failure. "If only HP knew what HP knows, we would be three times more productive", said Lew Platt, the former Chief Executive of Hewlett Packard. Continuous collection of word of mouth stories is a great way to stay sensitive to market changes and react to them swiftly. Such stories also allow you to see in what ways you can stand out.

Loves me, loves me not

Have you heard about the innovation consultancy Smart Design? They have come up with an ingenious method of not only collecting customer stories, but also capturing the sentiment behind them. The idea is as follows: instead of directly asking people what they liked or didn't like about a particular product, service or a brand, they asked customers to write a love letter or a breakup/divorce letter that was based on real-life experiences and interactions. This method was based on the assumption that we develop emotional attachments to whatever we use, be it a product, offering or a brand. And like any relationship, these relations have ups and downs of their own. So, it's not that hard for us to express our emotions towards them in the heat of the moment. Both good and bad. Try it yourself. Think of your bank or mobile provider, or a shop around the corner. What would you write if you were to let them know how you feel about them?

Play is a Polish telecom company that was taking the market by storm some years ago. Since the telecom market is a commodity market, the management board was looking for an alternative way to differentiate itself. Betting on delivering a great experience seemed like a good direction but the CMO asked, "Does a telecom business have a chance to become a love brand? Or are our services like tap water? Do customers develop an emotional attachment to a brand like ours? And if yes, what emotions do they express toward us?"

There was a good example to follow with respect to these questions. A Norwegian insurance company, Gjensidige, had decided some years earlier that they wanted to become a love brand.[128] I must admit, putting the words "love brand" and "insurance company" together in one sentence sounds a little unusual. The Norwegians seem to have thought the same. When, back in 2007, Gjensidige conducted the first study about the love brands in Norway, they found themselves to be ranked 77th. But the CEO, Helge Bairo Bastaad, declared, "We will be one of the top 10 most customer-focused organisations in Norway." It didn't matter that they had to compete with the automotive brands or grocery store chains. They chose to make it all the way to the shortlist of brands that are most loved by their customers. It took seven years and remodelling practically the entire business to become number 11. It sounded like the challenge Play telecom might be willing to take up.

Inspired by both the example of Gjensidige and the love and divorce letters idea of Smart Design, we decided to run a similar study for Play. We asked first 600 and then 1000 customers to think of a brand they loved and one they disliked. We then asked them to write a divorce letter to the disliked brand and a love letter to the brand they admired, and to score these two brands on a scale from 1 to 10. In this way we had a benchmark for the perception of the loved and the disliked brands. We then asked about Play. Once more, participants were invited to write a divorce letter, a warning letter or a love letter, together with a word of mouth story they shared with others, and then score the brand on the same scale.★ In this way we could see whether it was evoking emotions and what kind of emotions they were. We ended by asking customers to associate the emotion they felt using the Plutchik Wheel of Emotions.[129],★★

★　In this study, we have decided to expand on the initial methodology proposed by Smart Design by adding one more option: writing a warning letter. In this way we provide greater variety of choices, indicating that a relationship with a brand is a continuum.

★★　As humans we are able to experience over 34 000 different emotions. Through years of study, American psychologist Robert Plutchik distinguished eight primary emotions that form a foundation for all others: joy, sadness, acceptance, disgust, fear, anger, surprise and anticipation. The Wheel of Emotions is designed to help you understand the nuances of emotion and how emotions contrast with each other[130].

Love Brand

10

9.5 ·   Favourite Brand

7.3 ·   Play

6.4 ·   Competitor

1

Disliked Brand

The collected stories helped to reshape the company's strategy. They showed where the company was doing well and where it was failing. It enabled the company to define a set of differentiators and also to capture the aspects they were failing at.

Collecting word of mouth in the form of stories and letters is an amazing way to understand the current experience of your customers.[131],★ By asking them to share these stories with you, you invite your customers to be your community-based intelligence that senses the changes in the market for you. You can notice both positive and negative patterns, so you can see how your actions influence your perception rather than just receiving a sad or smiley face at the end of an interaction with your brand. Finally, collecting stories

---

★   The Cognitive Edge Institute developed probably the most powerful tool to date, SenseMaker, that enables you to effectively capture and analyse customer stories. I would highly recommend looking into it if you are interested in collecting word of mouth feedback.

helps you leverage serendipity. You design to collect accidental encounters that can ignite your creativity and innovation through non-linear repurposing of what you have found in your data. And last but not least, you can use the stories to create a sense of urgency towards the change you desire. What is this change? We will look into this next.

AN EXAMPLE OF A DIVORCE LETTER

"I can't stand your deceitful advertising. You promise things you're not able to deliver. You're just a cheat. You take old and long-standing customers for granted. I've wasted a huge amount of money because of you and I will never forgive you. I've never had trust in you, but this time you've overstepped the line. I can't wait to see our contract expire. I'll join the competitors with relief. One thing I regret is spending 20 years with you, wasted."

AN EXAMPLE OF A LOVE LETTER

"If it wasn't for your services, I wouldn't be able to call anyone. You're the best and I could not replace you with anyone better. I joined you a long time ago, but still, I can't get enough of you. You have far-reaching coverage, thanks to which I can always get through easily to anyone I want. Your services are top quality, you don't misuse your power and you have offers for any budget. You go to great lengths to make everyone feel at home with you. May it never change or, if so, it shall only change for the better."

CHAPTER THREE

Umami Vision

Have you ever considered why your organisation exists? Clearly, there is enough competition; your customers have plenty of choices, anyway. Even if you specialise in something, others do a reasonably good job too. Or maybe they are even better than you. There seems to be a dizzying array of brands out there to choose from. And these options are not that much different from each other (remember the market averaging effect we discussed earlier?)

"In a free-enterprise, private-property system, a corporate executive is an employee of the owners of the business. He has a direct responsibility to his employers. That responsibility is to conduct the business in accordance to their desires, which generally will be to make as much money as possible while conforming to the basic rules of society, both those embodied in law and those embodied in ethical custom."[132] This statement was written back in 1970 by Nobel-prize winner in economics, Milton Friedman, the father of the present form of capitalism; one that is exclusively focused on delivering the ultimate stakeholder value and on supporting next-quarter trading moves. In the words of Jack Welch, the former CEO of GE, a stakeholder-value-driven strategy is, in fact, "...a series of short terms."[133] This is a bit of a limited view of business, isn't it? It is a logic of appealing to immediate needs, without taking into account the systemic impacts of your products and services. Such an approach leads to creating corporate visions that are short-sighted, empty and lacking in inspiration. They become a corporate joke mocked by both employees and customers, as neither employees nor customers are ever driven by making rich people even richer. They are driven by knowing that their work and life has meaning.[134]

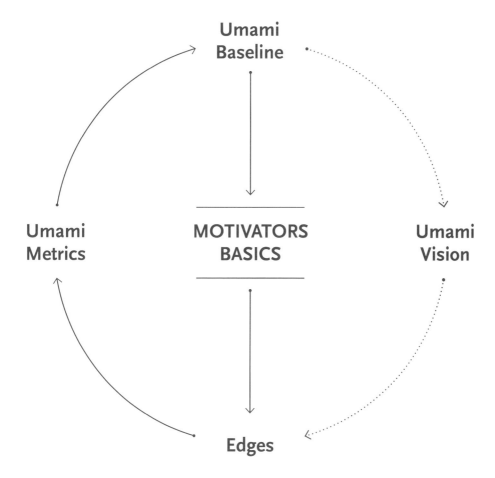

Consider the vision of McDonalds: "to move with velocity to drive profitable growth and become an even better McDonald's serving more customers delicious food each day around the world." What does this say about their purpose? Why do they exist in the first place? What it states is that the organisation is focused on generating as much value for stakeholders (drive profitable growth) as possible by bringing more and more people to their restaurants (serving more customers each day around the world). Note that they are saying that their food is delicious enough. Yeah, there is something to be said about becoming better but this point is suspiciously unspecific compared to the rest of that vision. So, what will the organisation focus on? The things that are crystal clear: bringing more people to McDonald's to generate more income.

Now, let's look at Nike. Their vision states: "Bring inspiration and innovation to every athlete in the world (if you have a body, you are an athlete)." They also add: "We dare to design the future of sport." There is nothing in this statement about increasing shareholder value. There is nothing about growing ever bigger at all costs. This vision statement attempts to answer the question stated by Theodore Levitt, in his influential book *Marketing Myopia* — why does your organisation exist in the first place?[135] For Nike it is about helping you to become as great an athlete as you can be. Their vision explicates that, rather than becoming ever richer, they aim to support anybody who would like to build their athleticism in ways that go beyond their core products. This is why, alongside their paid-for sportive attire, they offer products such as a training application or a meditation tool. They understand that their purpose allows them to create an ecosystem that goes beyond their core products and processes which, consequently, helps them to stay flexible with respect to how they address the challenge explicated in their vision.[136]

Your vision
Jim Collins called it a BHAG — a Big, Hairy, Audacious Goal.[137] There are two ways to look at such a goal. You could think of it as a "moon shot". A moon shot is something ambitious but achievable:

as J.F. Kennedy said in his address back in 1962, "We choose to go
to the moon. We choose to go to the moon in this decade and do
the other things, not because they are easy, but because they are hard,
because that goal will serve to organise and measure the best of our
energies and skills, because that challenge is one that we are willing
to accept, one we are unwilling to postpone, and one which we intend
to win, and the others, too." A lot of companies set their vision as
a moon shot. They say, we are going to be first or the biggest. But
the problem with a moon shot is that it primarily focuses on delivering shareholder value. Because what else is becoming the biggest or
the first? It is about getting as many people as possible to generate
your income. Obviously, companies exist to thrive financially. But
earning money is not a goal in itself. It is an effect, a measure of success showing that your vision inspires enough people to follow your
brand and to want you to exist in the first place.[138]

   This is why, instead of a moon-shot vision, you should have
something like what Simon Sinek calls a "just cause".[139] It speci-
fies higher order returns, returns that aim to positively impact
the world, be it the welfare of the customers, the community, society
as a whole or the well-being of our planet.[140] It defines the area you
want to improve through your existence. It is an expression of your
position with respect to the question, "Why do you exist in the first
place?" with a bigger and more meaningful answer that extends
beyond profit or financial return. It helps you stay focused on how
you want to change the world and who you want to change it for.
Patagonia has such a vision, something they call: "Our Reason for
Being." It states: "At Patagonia, we appreciate that all life on earth is
under threat of extinction. We aim to use the resources we have — our
business, our investments, our voice and our imaginations — to do
something about it."[141] This vision explicates that there is no end to
what Patagonia hopes to achieve. This vision is, in fact, more enduring than the organisation itself. This is why it is powerful, self-propelling and flexible at the same time.[142] It shapes the fundamental
choices Patagonia makes, and defines their subsequent milestones.
And what is even more crucial, it is a vision that is meaningful and

inspirational, both for the people inside and also outside of their organisation, which makes them the preferred brand for anyone who cares about the environment.

Think of such a vision as a journey to an unknown destination versus going to the place you have visited several times before. If you know your destination you are likely to develop tunnel vision: you will only see what you expect to see—things that advance you towards your goal. Why? Because if we know where we are going we tend to only see the things that advance us towards our destination.[143] In other words, we are likely to experience the confirmation bias—focusing on the information that confirms our chosen direction rather than looking for data that disproves our assumptions.[144] Yet, if you want to stand out you need to be the first to notice opportunities along the way that help you do things your competitors would never imagine doing. This is why an unachievable vision is a must. Think of it. If you travel to an unknown destination you are prone to see more for the simple fact that you need to keep orientating yourself and paying attention to where you are. And along the way you will discover things you didn't expect. These things are the basis of your differentiation.

One of my clients, Tylko, is a startup that designs and manufactures parametric furniture. They allow you to configure your fittings exactly the way you want. The company has been successful, but for a long time they felt that building furniture was not what they wanted to solely focus on.[145] What they dreamt of, in fact, was to stop over-consumption. With furniture? It sounds like a vision contradictory to their business, right? But if you consider that you can have furniture that lasts for a long time and can change with you, that helps you decide what is worth owning and what is not, suddenly the story starts to make sense. The only thing they needed was to dare to see their product (the parametric furniture) as a means to an end rather than an end in and of itself. Will Tylko stop over-consumption in the world? Probably not single-handedly. But they have the power to alter thinking about it. They have the power to start a movement. Or, at least, to contribute to one.

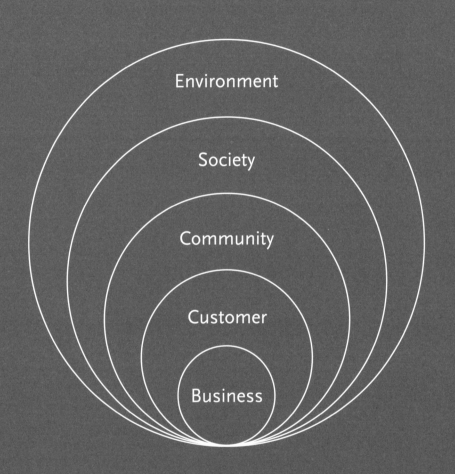

The Umami Vision is not about being first or being the fastest or cheapest; neither is it about having the biggest offer or the most customers. It is about asking yourself, "What kind of higher-order returns do you want the world to have tomorrow?"[146] You will recognise a great Umami Vision when you realise that it aims at building a world that doesn't yet exist. It needs to stem from your deep needs or passions, from something that is personally important to you and, at the same time, what your employees would subscribe to. So important that you are willing to do it at a cost of earning less money. If you have a vision that you don't have to trade anything for, it is not an Umami Vision. It can still be a good story to boost the company image or to put on your slides to present to your investors, but it won't be something that will excite your customers and motivate your employees.

Storytelling

Why is a vision needed in the first place? Having a vision is essential for a simple reason: its storytelling power is a way to convince first your employees and then your customers that you mean business when it comes to what you are aiming for. The evidence for this comes from neuroscience professor Uri Hasson at Princeton University. He and his team have shown that during storytelling, the storyteller's brain activity is mirrored in the listeners' minds—a phenomenon called "neural coupling".[147] So, if you are conveying your company vision and that vision takes the form of a story, it will help everyone in the organisation to empathise with it. And if you think about it, every organisation has such a story; its founding myth.[148]

Leg godt means "play well" in Danish, and Lego is made from the first two letters of each word. When naming his company, the founder Ole Kirk Christiansen was quite unaware that Lego in Latin means … "I put together". In 1988, the vision was explained by Kjeld Kirk Kristiansen in the form of the following statement: "We aim to inspire and develop the builders of tomorrow." Its ultimate purpose was (and still is) to help children think creatively, reason systematically and release their potential to shape their own future—experiencing endless human possibility.

From its founding in 1932 until 1998, the company had never posted a loss. But even amazing companies like Lego sometimes lose focus. By 2003 it was in big trouble. Sales were down 30 percent and it was 800 million dollars in debt. An internal report revealed it hadn't added anything of value to its portfolio for over a decade. Consultants advised diversification. The Lego brick had been around since the 1950s, they said, and it was obsolete. Lego should look to Mattel, a company whose toy portfolio was broad and varied. Following that advice, the company introduced jewellery for girls and Lego clothes. It opened theme parks that cost 140 million euros to build and lost 30 million euros in their first year. It built its own video-gaming company from scratch despite having no experience in the field.[149] It looked like the focus that had inspired the company for decades was lost.

"We are on a burning platform," the company CEO Jørgen Vig Knudstorp told his executives in 2001. "We're running out of cash... [and] likely won't survive." He decided to save Lego by going back to its initial vision. He dumped things the company had no expertise in.★ He slashed the inventory, halving the number of individual pieces Lego produced. He also encouraged interaction with Lego fans, something previously considered strictly prohibited. Lego launched its own crowdsourcing competition: originators of winning ideas would get one percent of their product's net sales, a competition which produced designs like the *Back to the Future* DeLorean time machine, the Beatles' *Yellow Submarine* and a set of female Nasa scientists.

By 2015, Lego announced profits of 760 million euros, making it the number one toy company in Europe and Asia, and number three in North America. From 2008 to 2010 its profits quadrupled, outstripping Apple's. Indeed, it has been called the Apple of toys: a profit-generating, design-driven miracle. And it was all because of the powerful, self-propelling "just cause" the company keeps focusing on.[150]

★   For example, the Legoland parks are now owned by the British company Merlin Entertainments.

In so many ways your Umami Vision is your dream. It helps you to see the shape of the end goal without marking one specific path to get there. Yet, even if you have a great vision, you might still fall into a number of traps. The biggest trap is that you might get lost in that vision and start day-dreaming, while doing the same thing over and over again. Or you might see the vision as so grandiose that it will become detached from your daily work. Or, even worse, you might believe that whatever you do will be okay as the vision is so grand, there is no way to see whether your present actions harm or nurture it.

Being too future-focused can make you immune to the small changes that happen today. They are simply so small compared to the big change you are hoping for that you don't appreciate them enough. So, in order to make your vision concrete enough for your organisation to be able to act upon, you need to define your ultimate customer — the customer that you want to make the most satisfied person in the world.

Finding your ultimate customer

If you ask around who the top priority customers are for big companies out there, I bet you that answer will be: "everybody". There seems to be a prevalent conception that if you are in the generic market, you need to deliver solutions that fit every single person. But, as we have already discussed before, nobody wants to be average. We all look for products, services, and experiences that make us feel special. The father of psychology, William James, remarked over 100 years ago that people consider their possessions to be a part of their self.[151] We use the things we have, the services we use and the brands we associate with as props for our self-presentation.[152] This is why Apple products are so successful — they appeal to our deep need for status in the social space. For this reason, so many of us (myself included) are willing to pay three times more for an Apple computer or an iPhone than for an alternative. Sure, it is easy to rationalise this choice: Apple products are more reliable, less prone to catching a virus and more sturdy, which is all true. But, besides all that, they look good and they make us look good.

The brands we use help us make sense of who we are and who we hope to become. This is why average offerings for average people are not at all attractive. Interestingly enough, as much as some companies seem to understand this phenomenon on the surface (by designing, for example, an unpacking experience), they somehow miss the deeper point, which is this: we are far more inclined to choose aspirational brands than we are those that are for "everybody".

There is one more problem with designing for an average customer: such customers don't seem to dream big. Their needs are rather basic and this is not very inspirational, either for the customers themselves or for the employees who are supposed to create something for them. But consider this: what would happen if you created an ideal future customer? Someone who is the ultimate in investing (for banks) or lives the healthiest life (for food brands)? Nike does exactly that—their entire brand experience makes you feel like you can become a great athlete even if you are currently a 100 percent couch potato.

Choosing an aspirational archetype has two major advantages. Firstly, it helps you define the best people you should talk to in order to see if you are advancing your vision. Think of Revolut. Their ultimate customer is a traveller, a person who moves from one place to another, uses multiple currencies, requires insurance and wants to rest at airports. Defining such an ultimate archetype helped Revolut create a very focused and therefore very powerful offer, one that is appreciated across the world. And it is appreciated because the customers who represent that archetype know what to expect and are willing to use the features like travel insurance or entry to the airport lounge, even if these services don't have that much to do with banking.

Secondly, focusing on aspirational customers will keep motivating your organisation to become a better version of itself. Let me bring back the example of Patagonia. Patagonia's focus on saving the planet makes it attractive to people who are environmentally aware. In turn, these people expect Patagonia to not only be consistent in their ways but also to be ambitious in how they want to impact the world. So, in other words, having an aspirational archetype of your ultimate customer is a way to change your organisational culture so that it remains focused on your vision.

Psychographics

For decades, it was considered good practice to segment your customers based on demographic and behavioural data. Demographic segmentation refers to segmenting your customers according to factors such as age, race, gender, family size, income or education. When an organisation defines behavioural segmentation, they evaluate the buying patterns of customers, like usage frequency, brand loyalty, or expected benefits. But here's the catch—neither demographics nor behaviour are satisfactory representations of your customers today.

The good news is that there is an alternative to this: psychographics.* It is, in fact, nothing new. In 1975, the *Journal of Marketing Research* published a paper titled "Psychographics: A Critical Review", in which advertising expert William D. Wells broke down what this emerging field was about.[153] He explained that psychographics aims to capture customer attributes such as personality, values, opinions, attitudes, interests, and lifestyle. Surely, it can be seen as yet another segmentation strategy in which the total market is divided based on psychology rather than demographics or behaviour. But its power lies in the ability to identify people based on the way they think and the kind of life they want to have. It is an effort to understand more deeply what motivates people's behaviour.[154] Using psychographics will help you to identify your ultimate customer and to create a portrait of what they are aspiring to become. This approach is successful to the degree that we can understand what our customers truly wish, what values are closest to their hearts and what intuitive associations shape the architectures of their minds.

★   You may have realised the power of psychographics from the Cambridge Analytica data scandal in early 2018. It revealed how Cambridge Analytica harvested personal data from Facebook profiles without the consent of its users and used it for political advertising purposes.

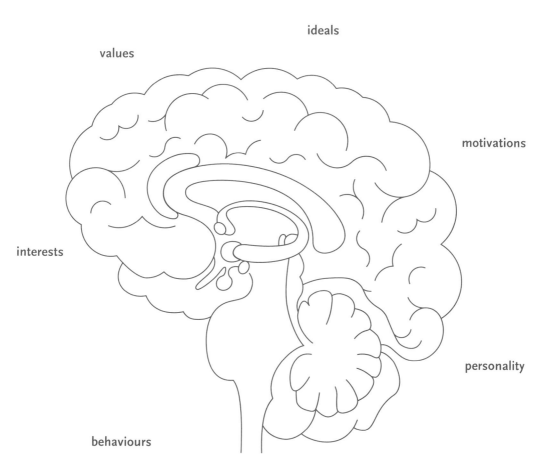

ideals

values

motivations

interests

personality

behaviours

life choices

CHAPTER FOUR
Umami Edges

Having a vision is a means to consolidate your efforts and help you reduce the level of uncertainty about where you are heading. Otherwise, you will never know whether you are on the right path. But having a vision is not enough. The problem with having a vision alone is that you can only see if it works with hindsight. Malcolm Campbell, an executive director of R&D division at Canon Medical, once said, "If you want to change the world you need two elements: you need to have the vision, which is the realm of imagination. And you have to figure out how you can implant this change into the current beliefs and ways of acting of people. Some guys are just visionaries. They live in the world of fantasy. Some are executioners — they know how to impose and execute something. Both are unlikely to succeed as in order to 'discern the course of fate' you need both those elements. You need to understand the change you want to bring about. And you need to act within the context you are in. Only then the change has a chance to be 'weaved into being'."[155]

To get started you need some ground rules: some indicators that show you and your stakeholders that you are, indeed, on the right track. Because if you want to be different, there won't be similar cases and examples you can follow. You are on your own and you are defining new standards here. This is why it is so important to choose what aspects you want to differentiate on, your edges; what Seth Godin calls, the ingredients for your "purple cow".[156] What is the "purple cow"? If you drive along a country road and you keep on seeing cows, you don't really see a particular cow. You just see a typical cow. If I were to ask you whether the last cow you saw was black or spotted white or brown, it's unlikely you would be able to remember. Unless you saw a purple cow. The sheer unlikelihood of seeing a purple cow would make you stop and

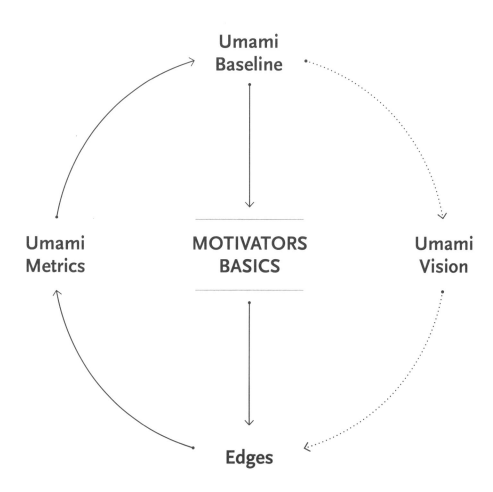

pay attention. This idea is similar for business. So, the edges are essentially the limits of your experiential approach, helping you to decide what you focus on when delivering solutions to your customers. If you don't have your edges, you are likely to fall into the trap of becoming heterogeneously homogenous. By choosing powerful edges and mercilessly executing on them, over time, you are likely to become a "purple cow".

Have you ever wondered why cars have two lights in front? It is an inheritance from the times when people used carriages pulled by horses for transportation. Typically, there were two horses pulling the carriage, each with a lamp hanging over their neck. So, when the first cars were built, the engineers equipped them with two lights so they resembled the traditional carriage. Now, have you ever wondered why there is a line to the checkout in so many stores? Apparently, historically this arises from the fact that before computerisation there was just one mechanical scale and one cash register in every shop. Nobody ever questioned that until Apple. Following their vision "Think Different", their shopping experience designers asked themselves: why should we have a line in the first place? Once they realised the reason behind it, it was easy to let go of this concept and to design the checkout experience anew. You could pick an item you wanted to purchase and approach any consultant in the store in order to pay. The consultant could use the iPod Touch equipped with a card reader to charge you. It was the first step towards becoming a "purple cow". But once Apple took that first step, it was even easier to make the next one. A few years later, if you had an Apple Store application, you were able to pick any item, scan the barcode with your app and leave, with no interaction with a consultant.[157] Your card would be automatically charged as you left the shop. Apparently, at first, some customers felt as if they were stealing phones and iPads. But over time they got used to the way the system worked and came to expect nothing less. This is called being edgy.*

★   According to *Collins Dictionary* being edgy means: "Following your dreams by overlooking the adversaries. It is about taking risks and always challenging yourself to be on the cutting edge."

When I talked to the designers of the Apple shopping experience a few years back, I asked, "How do your customers react to such alternative ways of shopping? Aren't they unhappy about it? Isn't it too unfamiliar?" My interlocutor Joanna, answered, "We educate our customers that we do things differently. So, they expect it from us. Actually, if we don't deliver a new concept for some time, they are disappointed and say that we are losing our edge." So, if you worry that being different is not going to be accepted by your customers, you might consider the way Apple does it. You can progress towards being edgy, towards standing out. It doesn't have to be done in one go. In order, to do so, you need to choose which aspects you want to be different in.

Find yourself an edge

The Economist wrote about Upmqua Bank: "An odd bank from an odd city doing oddly well." While most other banks across the globe prioritise becoming predominantly digital, Umpqua Bank considers two differentiators: Human + Digital. How is this strategy executed? Contrary to the global trend of limiting the number of branches, Umpqua keeps opening new ones. And these are not traditional branches at all. Aside from great coffee, local produce to purchase and authentic artwork on the walls (also by local artists), you can go there for yoga classes, book readings and theatrical performances. The offering is tailored to the needs of the surrounding community. For example, in one branch located near a home for the elderly, the manager hooked up a gaming console to large monitors hanging on the wall to create a popular virtual bowling league.

In addition, the bank has recently created a banking app called Go-To (cutely named BFF – Best Financial Friend – during its pilot stage). It allows its customers to instantly get in touch with their financial adviser over a video chat at any time and from anywhere. It enables them to conduct virtually every piece of business they could perform in a physical branch digitally, with the only exception being cash transactions. This focus on human touch is an example of a powerful differentiator; something that gets this particular bank noticed. Just as TYLKO battles overconsumption, Umpqua Bank wants to use banking to empower local communities. This is story-worthy, isn't it?

Think of Umami Vision as climbing Mount Everest. If you want to reach it there is more than one way to get there. You can take the "tourist" path from Kathmandu or you can approach it from the Tibetan side. Some of these roads are easier, some more difficult. You need to decide on the parameters of your path. This is what the edges are for. They should both reflect the motivators you want to focus on and also the most important basics you want to improve. Think of them as the adjectives describing the crucial qualities of your customers' experience, qualities you want to differentiate yourself on. They are your competitive choices and they aim to pre-empt your rivals in the aspects they don't expect.

DailyStrength is a social networking platform, where users provide one another with emotional support by discussing their struggles and successes with each other. It contains online communities that deal with different medical conditions or life challenges such as depression, divorce, parenting, or cancer. The company goal is to help anyone with life challenges in two aspects: "to simply and easily communicate their progress with friends, family, supporters, and have people to respond with encouragement and help" and "to help find others facing the same circumstances, and exchange experiences, treatments and even hugs within a safe community setting." These two rules explicate the edges of DailyStrength, which are: relatedness, support, encouragement and simplicity. As you can see, the first three represent motivators: safety, empathy and engagement, while the final edge captures one of the basics: usability. Having such a precise way of defining what DailyStrength is about helps them stay focused on the most important aspects of their service, determining their priorities.

Edges can be mistaken for company values but there is an important difference between them. Company values are the fundamental beliefs upon which your business and its behaviour are based. They are the guiding principles that your business uses to manage its internal affairs as well as its relationship with customers. Once set, your core values need to be firm and unwavering—a mandate rather than a suggestion. They should affect every aspect of your business, from employee benefit packages and workplace culture to marketing strategies and customer service.

Edges are your experiential differentiators. They are the qualities of your brand and your offering that make you stand out. They are the characteristics that need to be radically consistent across every touchpoint in the interaction with your customers. Think again about the Umpqua Bank. Their edges of being human + digital determine the ways they design their solutions. They are the guiding principles and the constraints at the same time. You can think of them as the type of path you choose to reach your vision. The edges should reflect the company values but the company values are a broader concept in that sense.

Edges play a twofold role for your strategy. On the one hand, they are the intermittent success markers along the road to reach your vision. They help your stakeholders see the progress and they give you and your employees a sense of success. Edges are also a way to give your vision momentum. They help you see if things are moving or stagnating. Finally, edges are a way to help you question the *status quo* as they focus your questions (as in the case of Apple). And since they are more short-term oriented and more concrete compared to your vision, they offer you a sense of completion.

Edges as your principles

Just as company values should not be merely stated but also practised, the same applies to your edges. Edges define your competitive advantage and determine your strategy. They are heuristics for your experience design, your rules of conduct. Focusing rules through the lens of your edges allows you to pay attention to the most critical variables and ignore any factors that introduce noise to your decision-making process. But above all, they offer you the space for creativity and innovation, as they do not exclude new ways of thinking.

Before the Aeron chair, office chairs were, well, just chairs. It was hard to see any difference between one chair and another. Then, in 1994, came Herman Miller with his over 1000-dollars-worth proposition. It was a risky product on all accounts. It looked different, worked differently and was insanely expensive compared with the market average. But at the same time, it was edgy. With a frame of high-tech moulded plastic, a skin of woven plastic fibres and mechanics that accommodated slouchy rebels, it was a Purple Cow. Built for their ultimate customer, a Sillicon Valley start-up founder, this chair sent a message about who you were and what you did if you sat in it. Millions of Aeron chairs have been sold since then and the chair itself is part of the permanent collection at the Museum of Modern Art. What were its edges? "The best design solves problems but if you weld that to a cool factor then you have a home run", said Mark Schurman, the director of corporate communications. Extreme comfort and extreme coolness seemed to have worked out greatly for Herman Miller.

As well as becoming your principles, edges also serve as your constraints. You might think that having constraints is bad. But it is the opposite. Think of any sport—they are all based on constraints. The way we play tennis follows a set of rules, which are nothing more but constraints. They give the game its character, its energy and determine the pleasure you get out of it. Constraints restrict us in our behaviour, but at the same time, they help us differentiate from others.[158] Think of constraints as the rules depicting what you are *not* going to do in order not to damage your vision and edges. They are your tools for sharpening your focus and a foundation for innovative thinking. Applying constraints makes you adapt your solutions in new ways, much as evolution works.[159] Constraints force you to keep asking, "What is this for?" or "Why is this the best form for such a function?" Think about Twitter with its 140-character limit to any message—this very constraint made it successful and different from blogs. Another example is Whole Foods. They have defined two groundbreaking constraints: no artificial flavours and no artificial colours. They illustrated these constraints by creating an inventory of "unacceptable ingredients" or even "unacceptable food categories" (such as chips or candy), which they guard against. By limiting themselves to sourcing only natural products, the company became a symbol of wellness and healthy living. So, you can see edges as your principles or your constraints, as long as they serve as leverage to differentiate you in the market. Leveraging your edges helps you stay inventive and encourages you to avoid the common way of doing things; to create your own distinct ways of doing things.

Choosing your edges

Your edges are your choice and your choice only. But there are two aspects that are important to remember when you define them. Firstly, avoid edges that your competition is already excelling at. The effort required to truly stand out in this aspect will be very costly. Let's say your competition is excellent at delivering an instant reaction to customer communication. Of course, you should make sure your response time is adequate but are you truly going to differentiate yourself if your email arrives a little faster? Would your customers even notice? Probably not. It might be much better to create your own unique communication style, like UK-based online printing-house Moo does. Instead of sending the regular confirmation emails so many other businesses do, they do this:

Hello Aga,
I'm Little MOO — the bit of software that will be managing your order with moo.com. It will shortly be sent to Big MOO, our print machine who will print it for you in the next few days. I'll let you know when it's done and on its way to you.
If you've imported your images to MOO from another site, please make sure you don't remove or change the photos you've chosen from that site until this order has been printed, or some pictures may come out blank. (If you've uploaded them directly to MOO, then there's no need to worry.)

Thanks,
Little MOO, Print Robot

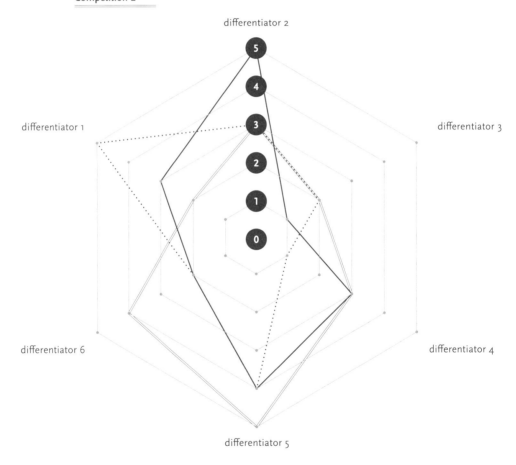

It may seem like nothing special but, believe me, when you get this email you will notice. And you will talk about it.

Secondly, your edges should reflect qualities that are irresistible to your ultimate customer. Revolut CEO, Nikolay Storonsky, says, "We're trying to build a 10 times better financial services company that is 10 times cheaper as well... the only way to do it is not building only one product, but building a platform with a lot of products on top of it."[160] This platform is becoming "an Amazon for banking" for one reason only: it is created to consistently serve its ultimate customer — the Traveller. It is a great example that shows the power of aligning your edges with the needs and aspirations of your ultimate customer group makes you stand out in a crowded market.

How do you choose your differentiators? First of all, it is crucial to understand how these edges relate to and strengthen your vision. Then you need to ask yourself: are they challenging enough to provoke you to move away from the current path? Some companies choose differentiators that cement their current way of thinking rather than spur an innovative approach. It is good to choose edges that contrast with the way you and others conduct business today. They should be provocative enough to stir innovative thinking across your organisation. It is also worth asking yourself: "are these qualities exciting enough for our employees?" If your employees are not going to be animated because of them, they will be unlikely to deliver what you are hoping for. And finally, you should check that these qualities don't undermine your financial goals. It is wise to choose edges that will not be thrown out of the window once you need to turn in your financial report.

How many edges should you choose? You shouldn't go for just one (more about this in the next chapter). Two core edges are easy for everyone in your organisation to remember and they are also a great tool for selecting which ideas to follow through with. You might call them your extremes. For example, you might decide that you want to be extremely playful (an edge representing the motivator: fun) and extremely trustworthy (the edge representing the basic: reliability). If you feel that two is not enough, you might select additional supportive edges: they are not as vital as your main two but they help you to become more subtle with your approach (in other words, they provide the extra spice to your projects).

There is one last thing worth remembering. As Seth Godin points out—the opposite of being edgy is being very good. Being just one step ahead. Being just a little bit better will keep you within the Zone of Tolerance, making the experience not very memorable for your customers. If you go to a restaurant that offers you just a regular meal, you are not going to think about it twice, let alone share it with others. You need to be extreme to be story-worthy. Because good and very good is pretty much the reality today. And nobody is going to waste a moment talking about it.

The balancing act

So, now you have your edges. Now, it's time to pick your battles. Following the words of W. Edwards Deming, "It is not enough to do your best; you must know what to do and then do your best." It is crucial to know what principles and constraints you are putting in your path, otherwise you might easily get lost. The number one challenge is to explicate what your edges mean for *you*. Let's come back to the example of Umpqua Bank and their edges of being human and digital. What do these mean to them? They could ask themselves: do we want the primary purpose of our business to be to serve individual customers? Are we delivering affordable or premium services? Do we create an ecosystem or are we focusing on a more independent product portfolio? These might be some of the dilemmas your business faces. You need to find them, name them, prioritise them and (crucially!) define what they mean.

The phrase "the balancing act" was first coined by Franco Bianchini and Charles Landry as a way of specifying the poles of policy issues in an urban context (where examples of the extremes were "no state intervention in the cultural sector" versus "government control of cultural resources").[161] As much in the context of policy making as in the context of business, you will rarely find yourself choosing one or the other extreme. You will most likely place yourself somewhere between the two poles, depending on your circumstances.

The value of identifying the extremes lies in being able to see your own position in relation to them. Are you in the middle? Or closer to a 60–40 split, a 90–10 split, or a 30–70 split? Since they are dilemmas, it is unlikely that you will clearly identify yourself on one side of the scale.[162] If you do this exercise with a group of people, you will find out soon enough that your opinion might differ from the opinions of others. It is a trigger for a discussion that ultimately leads to making a list of things that you do and you don't do as a company. This is how you translate your edges into a set of principles: the high-level guiding heuristics that help you set the boundaries to your actions, outputs and outcomes.

Business clients	....	Individual clients
Premium	....	Affordable
Stationary	....	Mobile
Narrow product offering	....	Broad product offering
Time to market	....	Quality first
Ecosystem	....	Independent products

CHAPTER FIVE
Umami Metrics

According to the UN, 2.5 billion people around the world lack access to a toilet. As a result, human faeces ends up on the roadside, in drinking water and eventually in people's digestive systems. The outcome is dysentery, which kills more than 4000 children per day. Actually, diseases spread by waste kill more people worldwide every year than any other single cause of death.[163] Rose George, author of *The Big Necessity*, a book which breaks the taboo about bodily waste, points out that "waste" is a poorly chosen phrase as human faeces is an excellent source of nutrients and energy. Its value may be alien to those of us living in Western societies but in parts of the world where access to decent sanitation is limited and opportunities for finding a sustainable energy source slim, reusing human waste can present valuable possibilities. This is what the LooWatt team noticed and decided to explore.

LooWatt is a startup whose vision is to create physical, emotional and environmental wellbeing through waterless sanitation. Their odourless toilets use a sealing mechanism to wrap human waste in a biodegradable liner that is pulled through a sealer when the toilet is flushed. The "cartridge" is then emptied into an anaerobic digester, where the waste and biodegradable liners are converted into biogas and fertiliser.

Back in 2012, while still students at Imperial College in London, the LooWatt team received a 100 000 dollar investment from the Bill & Melinda Gates Foundation to run a trial for their product in the capital of Madagascar, Antananarivo. When giving them the cheque, Melinda said, "If you succeed in the next 14 months to bring more health to Africa, we will give you a million dollars." Nick Coutts, who

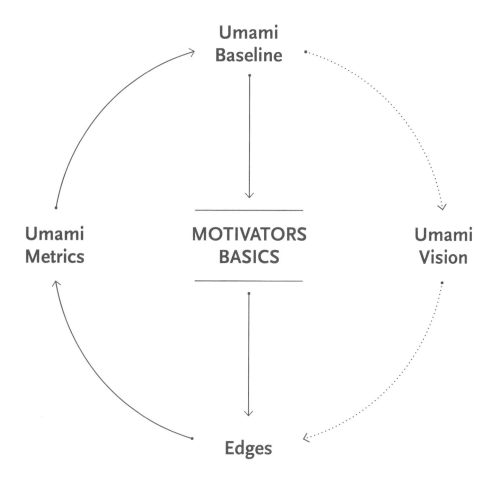

was an advisor for the team, suggested, "If you want to make sure you are getting your million bucks, you should learn how to measure what's important."

The team decided to call upon Tom Gilb, the creator of the Evolutionary Project Management and Product Development method (EVO).[164] If you have ever heard Tom speaking, you will know that he is a firm believer that everything can (and should) be measured. Tom spent one day with LooWatt, first quantifying the objectives that were important for the foundation and then prioritising the projects LooWatt founders were considering against those objectives. Before this exercise took place, the team was determined to focus on the product itself. The exercise with Tom helped them to better understand what the long-term health objectives for Madagascar were in the eyes of the foundation (like sustainability and longevity of the provided solutions, risk management and diffusion of knowledge), and concentrate their efforts to address the aspects that lay at the heart of the foundation's mission. Fourteen months later the startup was awarded more than one million dollars for further development of their idea.[165] Knowing what was important and how to measure progress was key to that success.

What are metrics for?

Progressing toward your long-term vision and building a reputation as an outstanding brand will happen only if you keep on delivering the right results. If you are to do so you need to carefully select the most important things to focus on as early as possible. If you manage to generate success early on, it will allow you to keep going in the direction you want to.[166] The only way to stay focused is to use metrics to aid you in making decisions, to help you figure out what works so you can do more of it, and to verify your progress. ★

★   My favourite definition of measurement comes from Douglas Hubbard: "Measurement is a qualitatively expressed reduction of uncertainty based on one or more observations."

In other words, the ultimate goal of good metrics is to reduce uncertainty to the point where you feel confident in selecting one course of action to meet your goals with the least effort and using the least amount of resources.★

Today's perception of what metrics are for is rooted in the statement allegedly attributed to Peter Drucker, "What doesn't get measured, doesn't get done." This statement implies that people predominantly respond to incentives (which is not necessarily what Drucker meant). And if an incentive is not attached to a certain goal, people won't do it. Hence, whenever things go wrong, organisations tend to define new measures as a way to obtain new tools for possible punishment (and more rarely, reward). In other words, the vast majority of measures today serve as a proverbial "stick and carrot". As a consequence, they provoke thinking in terms of: "What can I do that will get me the best result?", rather than thinking: "What can we do to create the most value?"

Being truly numbers-driven begins with a common understanding of what we mean by those numbers and how we define success. But it also means that we know when we failed and lost. Therefore, good metrics should have three qualities. They must be:

- relevant, which means focused on your vision and your edges;

- powerful, which means that they stimulate creativity; and

- useful, which means that they are concrete enough to become actionable.

★   For those of you who wonder where this definition comes from, it is based on the Bayesian interpretation of probabilities.

Finally, good metrics should be set up not to command and control people but to inspire, align and focus them. They should measure the value of the experience you want to deliver (among other things that are relevant to business). And measuring value is tough because it requires both staying visionary and applying analytical and precise thinking at the same time.

The value of multiple measures

Back in the 1980s, a number of prominent American hospitals agreed on a single measure of their medical proficiency: the patient mortality rate. It was supposed to give patients insight into information that they had never before been privy to. It soon became evident that the function of mortality rate was, in fact, a combination of different factors, including the type of patients admitted, the kinds of experimental research and the level of care the hospital provided. The best way for a hospital to receive a high score was to stop admitting the sickest patients. Setting just one generic measure led to the opposite effect from the intended one. Instead of providing the best possible care for those patients who needed it the most, the hospitals were inclined to reject them and send them to a potentially worse place. In this sense, the measure fell prey to what the British anthropologist Marilyn Strathern (paraphrasing Goodhart's Law) said, "When a measure becomes a target, it ceases to be a measure at all." No matter how well-intended, a single measure is often too generic to produce useful results.[167]

There was a glass bottle manufacturer in the south of Poland in the 1980s. For a long time, they made two kinds of bottles (first and second sort). At some point, the management decided that they didn't want to produce the second-sort bottles anymore. They gave a target: a 100 percent reduction in the production of second-sort bottles, and they attached a financial reward to reaching that objective. One month later, not a single second-sort bottle was produced. The management were happy because they could see how well their strategy worked, and the employees were happy because they got their reward. A year later, a new client came who enquired about the second-sort bottles.

The management went down to the work floor and asked, "What would it take to start producing them?" "Nothing", was the answer, "We just stop breaking them." So, apart from the fact that your single measurement can, in fact, measure the wrong thing, it can also be cheated. It may give you a false perception of success but it doesn't mean that that success is real. In fact, you might not be on the path to the success you were hoping for at all.

Finally, a single measure runs the risk of not accounting for the possible side-effects your actions can have on your visions and edges. Recently, I went to a sports shop to buy a shirt and a pair of flip-flops. As I was walking around, I heard two announcements. One said, "Our brand stands for being fair." The other said, "We have a promotion today — if you purchase two items from our clothing or shoe assortment, you will receive a 20 percent discount on both items." With one shirt and one pair of flip-flops, I approached the counter. The casher charged the full price on both items. Curious, I enquired as to why the promotion was not applicable. "It doesn't apply to flip-flops. And it doesn't apply to this collection of shirts either", the cashier answered, looking at me apologetically, and added that she felt embarrassed by the restrictions. Obviously, the promotion had small print attached to it. Which, apart from leaving me with a feeling of disappointment, was proof that this brand most likely had one metric: the financial one. They had calculated what made this particular offer financially reasonable and hadn't considered what impact it would have on the customer perception of how fair they were. If they had at least considered two metrics, the fairness *and* the finances, they might have been able to realise that by setting their promotion in the way they did, they unintentionally damaged the perception of being fair. Having just one metric made them blind and the metric itself was not helping them build the brand image they were hoping for.

If you are after a measurement tool that is relevant, powerful and actionable, it is crucial that you put not just one but a few measures together to guide your decisions and actions. Having a set of metrics further helps you to diagnose what possible side effects might occur with respect to the solution you are implementing.

There is one final reason why you should have multiple metrics rather than just one. As humans, we all tend to make decisions based on our intuition.[168] Taking intuitive decisions has advantages: it is fast and it gives you a feeling of being an expert. But there's a problem with this. Our intuitions are usually not very good. What's even worse, if your intuitive decision was wrong in the first place, you will keep on looking for arguments that confirm it rather than correct it (it is called the "confirmation bias"). Daniel Kahneman compares it to having a bunch of witnesses and allowing them to speak to each other. The result will be significantly less reliable than if you separated each witness and talked to them individually. Having multiple metrics as a decision-making algorithm will delay your inevitable intuition and slow down your judgment. It will enable you to integrate the information you have before deciding what to do. If you have to look at a given solution from multiple angles, you will have a multifaceted perspective before making your final decision. And this is the key to the success of your strategy, as it makes you assess the objective tradeoffs rather than defending personal impressions.

More stories like this

In previous sections we looked at the topic of measurement as a whole. I will focus now on how it applies to your experience strategy. In the traditional metrics of customer engagement (the Net Promoter Score) the most common measure is to count how many people would be willing to recommend your brand to others. The eyes of executives are focused on that question. The answer is given in the form of a numerical scale. Of course, it is crucial to know whether your customers are willing to advocate for your brand or discourage others from using it. But, as much as knowing if you are to be recommended or not, you need to understand the reasons why your customers recommend you in the first place. Paraphrasing the words of the founder of the Cognitive Edge Institute, Dave Snowden, you need to select which stories you would like to amplify through your actions and which stories you'd rather stop from being told.

InPost is a delivery company whose vision is to enable you to receive a package as quickly as possible, whenever and wherever you want. They are known for their uniquely cute communication style and for their extreme focus on efficiency. Stories about them are typically concerned with how fast and easy it was to send or receive a package and how funny their text messages and emails were. So, it seems that extreme efficiency and extreme cuteness are the edges this company is after.

Let's think now about how their Umami Metrics could be constructed. Their progress towards their vision could be expressed though customer narratives similar to stories such as this: "Using InPost feels like having your packages teleport to the place you want to" or, "This is the most convenient way to send and receive packages." What kind of stories would reflect their edges? When it comes to extreme efficiency, they might be looking for stories like: "There is no more efficient way to send and receive my package" or, "There is no other way to send and receive things that's easier to use." The extreme cuteness could be expressed through statements such as: "I love to receive messages from InPost. They always make me smile" or, "I was almost sad that the interaction ended." Such stories are expressions of whether the company is going in the direction it wants to.

So, for InPost, their metrics could be defined in terms of the stories their customers tell and these stories, in fact, create rows for their measurement tool: the Umami Table. Next to the Umami Metrics, they could add other metrics that are crucial for their business (like EBIDTA★ or the development effort). In this way, they have a comprehensive set of measures that enables them to assess and then prioritise their projects and initiatives, but most importantly, the decision makers have the same frame of reference for discussions.

★   EBIDTA is a business term for earnings before interest, depreciation, taxes, and amortisation.

UMAMI METRICS (more stories like this)

....

"Using InPost feels like having your packages teleport to the place you want to."
(a type of story representing the company vision)

....

"There is no more efficient way to send and receive my package."
(a type of story representing the extreme efficiency)

....

"I love to receive messages from InPost. They always make me smile."
(a type of story representing the extreme cuteness)

BUSINESS METRICS

....

EBIDTA

....

Growth of customer base

....

Implementation cost

....

...

Selecting the most important next thing to do

Once you have your Umami Table things get fairly easy. Your metrics form the rows of that table and your initiatives are its columns. Every initiative can have negative, positive or neutral impact on each individual measure.★ In the Umami Table I've marked the negative impact using up to three minuses, and up to three plusses for positive impact. To see the overall impact of a given initiative, you simply add up the pluses and the minuses. If you add the implementation cost to the table, you will have a fairly good picture of which initiative shows great promise and which should be abandoned.

I suggest two guiding rules when working with your Umami Table. The first is: no initiative is accepted if it negatively impacts your vision. In other words, if you see that there is even one minus next to the metric that estimates the progress towards your vision (in this case the vision is represented by the statement: "Using InPost feels like having your packages teleport"), you reject that initiative, no questions asked, or you fix it so it no longer hurts your vision. Having that rule is crucial because it shows your commitment to your vision. And, as I mentioned earlier, only if you follow your vision will your employees and customers be willing to engage with you emotionally and, consequently, follow you.

Another rule is: if one initiative harms one of your edges, you will launch another initiative that has at least an equalising positive impact on that edge to compensate for the negative impact. You could also decide that if an initiative has an overall positive impact on the Umami Metrics but is not financially beneficial, you will see it as a project promoting your brand. And so on. How many rules you need is for you to decide but if you have them, they will help you make informed decisions on what you should do and what you shouldn't.

★ This is the first step of a much larger methodology called EVO proposed by Tom Gilb (who I mentioned when talking about LooWatt). If you'd like to dig deeper, check out his writings on his website.[169] They are not an easy read but the approach proposed by Tom is very comprehensive and will get your company aligned from top to bottom.

UMAMI TABLE

		initiative 1	initiative 2	initiative 3
UMAMI METRICS	"Using InPost feels like having your packages teleport to the place you want to." (a type of story representing the company vision)	+ +	+	+ + +
	"There is no more efficient way to send and receive my package." (a type of story representing the extreme efficiency)	+ +	+	+ + +
	"I love to receive messages from InPost. They always make me smile." (a type of story representing the extreme cuteness)	0	+ + +	+
	IMPACT OF EXPERIENCE	4	5	7
BUSINESS METRICS	EBIDTA	+	+	+ +
	Growth of customer base	+	+ +	+ + +
	BUSINESS VALUE	2	3	5
	IMPLEMENTATION COST	70 000	115 000	250 000
	Return on Investment (the sum of experience impact and business value divided by the implementation cost)	9	7	5

This approach can be scaled throughout your entire organisation. For example, if you are the logistics department of InPost you might divide these generic statements into the measures that are relevant to your day-to-day work. For example, extreme efficiency might mean aiming at improving the average time of collecting a package by 10 percent. And you may well assume that cute communication is not something you will be working on — it will be taken care of by one of your sister teams. On the other hand, if you are the leader of the application development team, you might both look after simplifying and speeding up the posting and collecting of the package, and on making your communications positively surprising and engaging. So, you create your own table that guides your projects and helps you prioritise them. Understanding how each project links to your strategy gives you a powerful alignment tool.[170] At the same time, the Umami Table gives you the freedom to select what is the next most important thing to focus on that is left in the hands of the teams.

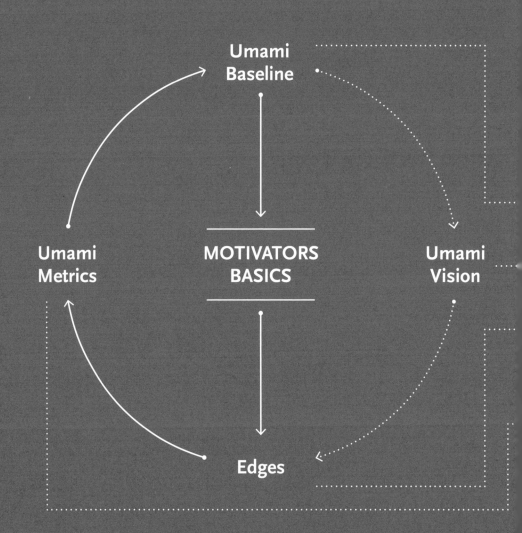

Umami
Baseline

Umami
Metrics

MOTIVATORS
BASICS

Umami
Vision

Edges

Practical Tools for Your Umami Strategy

1. Umami Baseline Questionnaire

What, do you think, would your customers write to you if they got an opportunity to write you a letter? Would it be a love letter or a divorce letter? Or perhaps a warning? What story would they share about you? This questionnaire outline aims to inspire you to create a survey that could become your Umami Baseline. It consists of three elements: benchmarking your brand against other loved and disliked brands, capturing the emotions of your customers and collecting the stories they share about you. Each of these elements (or a combination of them) has the potential to become your research tool for setting your Umami Baseline.

> GOAL: Capture word of mouth and the sentiment towards the experience you offer.

Benchmarking against other love brands:

1. Think of a brand you truly admire and a brand you heavily dislike.

2. Rank them on a scale from 1 to 10, where 1 means heavily disliking the brand and 10 means having a strong positive feeling towards the brand.

3. Write a love letter to the brand you like and a divorce letter to the brand you dislike.

4. Describe a situation that made you like or dislike that brand.

5. Rank your brand and your two biggest competitors on the same scale in relation to the loved and the disliked brand.

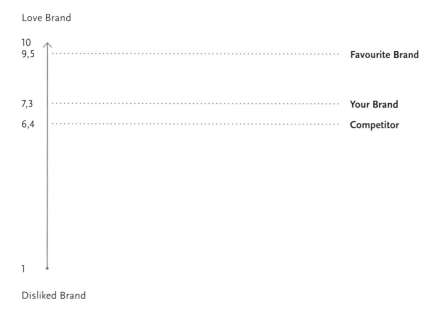

Love Brand

10
9,5 .... **Favourite Brand**

7,3 .... **Your Brand**
6,4 .... **Competitor**

1

Disliked Brand

Collecting customer stories:

1. Write a story (of minimum six sentences) that you shared with others about the brand.

2. Using the Wheel of Emotions (see page 137), mark the emotion that is reflected in your story. On a scale from 1 to 10, how strong was that emotion?

3. Answer the following questions:
   • how many people did you share this story with?
   • who were these people—family, friends, acquaintances, strangers?
   • how long have you been telling this story to others?

Capturing the customer sentiment toward your brand:

1. Write a love, warning or divorce letter to the brand (at least three sentences).

2. If you were to view the brand as a person, what would be the strongest emotion you feel towards it?

3. If this were a personal relationship, what kind of relationship would it be (a friend, a partner, an acquaintance, an enemy or perhaps a clerk)?

4. Answer the following questions:
   - how long have you been with that brand?
   - have you ever considered switching to another brand? If yes, which?
   - what arguments would convince you to stay with that brand?

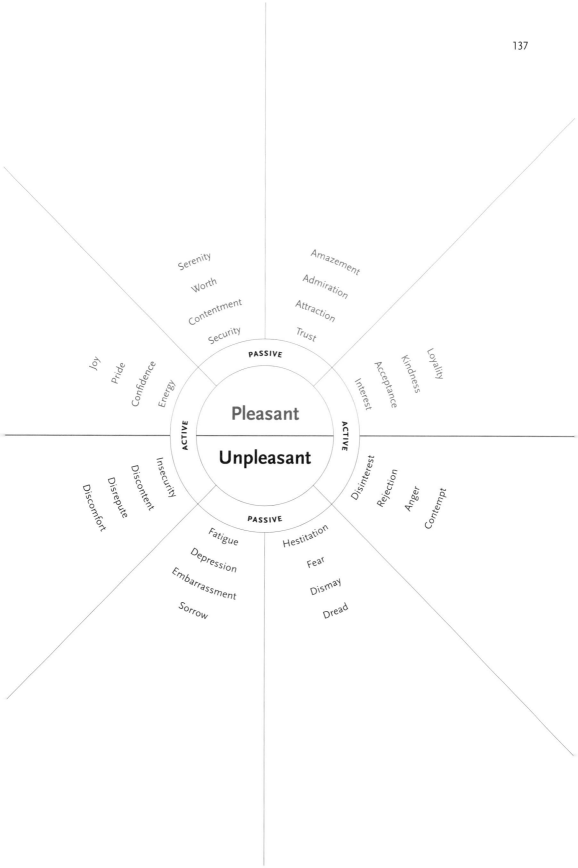

2. Umami Progress Questionnaire

The Umami Baseline Questionnaire creates a baseline that should be run regularly so that you can keep an eye on the stories your customers tell about your brand. But once you define your vision and your edges, it would also be good to test how your customers see you progressing towards these. This is why it would be wise to add two additional elements to your original Umami Baseline Questionnaire, enquiring about the vision and the edges.

| GOAL: Assess your progress towards your vision and edges.

Evaluating progress towards the Umami Vision:
     A good way of evaluating your vision is to prepare a set of statements related to your Umami Vision (these can come from the vision statements of your competitors or other brands you admire). So, for example, if your brand mission is to stop overconsumption, you could propose the following statements.

Brand X is in the business of:
- making furniture,
- beautifying the world,
- stopping overconsumption,
- challenging the *status quo*,
- delivering happiness.

Then you ask your customers the following:

1. Choose the statement that in your eyes best describes Brand X.

2. If you were to assess from 1 to 10 (when 1 indicates a little, and 10 indicates a lot), how successfully do you think is Brand X fulfilling that statement?

3. Once you make your decision, explain in a few sentences your reasons why.

Evaluating progress towards the edges:

If you want to assess your progress towards your edges, one way to do so is to define a set of sliders consisting of your edges with their positive antonyms. So, if for example, your two main edges are: extreme playfulness and extreme effortlessness and you also have supporting edges such as familiarity, mobility and surprise, your set of sliders would look like this:

Then ask your customers the following:

1. Using the slider, evaluate which of these qualities best describe Brand X.

2. Once you make your decision, explain in a few sentences your reasons why.

You can run this exercise to track your overall progress and you can also use it for evaluating individual projects.

3. The Aspiration Map

The aspiration map is a collaborative tool to help you get a deeper insight into the psychographics of your customers. The map aims to depict a group of users with similar personality traits, values, lifestyle choices and behaviours. It is inspired by the empathy map originally created by Dave Gray. The aspiration map can be used whenever you need to define your ultimate customer group and relate it to the different customer groups found among people using your offering.

| GOAL: Define the psychographic profile of your ultimate customer.

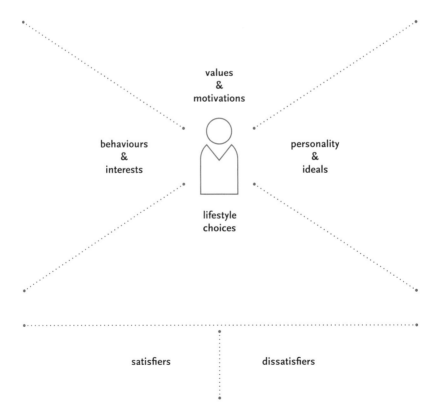

1. Gather your team and bring all the research data you have about the target group for your aspiration map.

2. Sketch the aspiration map template on a large piece of paper or a whiteboard.

3. Hand out the list with the following questions to each participant to help them generate insights for the map:

   • What are the main personality traits for this customer group? What do they believe in? What are their ideals? What change do they want to see in the world? What are they sceptical about? What are they against?

   • What are their values? What are the things they would never give up on? What drives their actions and reactions? What demotivates them?

   • What are their life choices? What kind of lifestyle do they prefer? What wouldn't they ever give up? What doesn't matter much to them? What are they happy to live without?

   • What attitudes do they display towards products and offerings? What is important to them? What is unimportant? What does motivate them when it comes to choosing products and offerings? What are their purchase behaviours? What are their usage behaviours?

   • What makes a solution satisfying for them?

   • What makes it dissatisfying?

4. Give each participant a set of sticky notes and a sharpie. Each person should write down their thoughts on stickies, one thought on each sticky. Use research data to inspire and justify your statements.

5. Ask each participant to share what they wrote on their stickies and why. Then place the stickies on the map.

6. Based on the map list ten core aspirations for your ultimate customers.

7. Generate hypotheses regarding what would be the appealing solutions for them and then validate these ideas with real users.

4. The Five Whys Revisited

Powerful questions help you reframe your thinking. Perhaps the most well-known questions when it comes to thinking about your vision are: "What business are we in?" asked by Theodore Levitt in his famous HBR article "Marketing Myopia" and "Why do you do what you do?" by Simon Sinek in his book *Start With Why*. I always add one extra question that complements these two, which is: "Why is it important?"

Each of these questions should be asked more than once. This was the reason behind the creation of the Five Whys exercise at Toyota popularised by Taiichi Ohno, the architect of the Toyota Production System. Five Whys is an iterative technique used to explore the cause-and-effect chain underlying a given opinion.

| GOAL: Define your umami vision.

1. Prepare two sheets. On sheet 1 write five times: What business are we in? Why is it important? On sheet 2 write five times: What value are we bringing to the world? Why is it important? Leave space for writing the answer below each question.

2. Divide yourselves into pairs: Person A and Person B. Person A gets sheet 1 and Person B gets sheet 2.

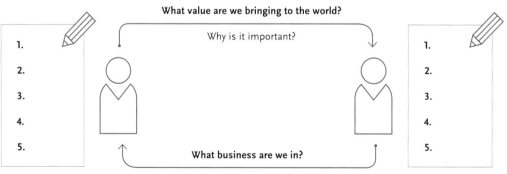

3. In each pair, Person A takes the question: "What business are we in?" They ask this question of Person B five times from five different perspectives: your business, your customers, the community surrounding you, the society you are a part of and the environment you function in (consider both the immediate environment and the planet as a whole). Each time, after Person B answers the first question, Person A asks the additional one: "Why is it important?" Person A notes the answers of Person B to both questions.

4. Then Person B takes the question: "What value do we bring to the world?" They repeat the procedure – Person B asks this question of Person A five times from the five above-mentioned perspectives: your business, your customers, the community surrounding you, the society you are a part of and the environment you function in. Each time, Person B adds the additional question: "Why is it important?" after the main question is answered. Person B notes Person A's answers to both questions.

5. Once you have all answers collected, come together as a group and analyse them. Write down a vision statement consisting of three or four sentences. You could use the Purpose Pyramid to help you formulate them.

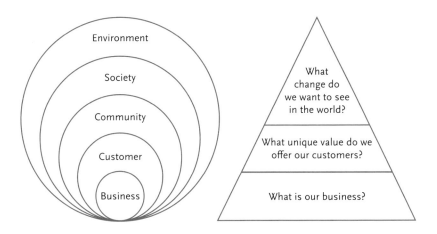

5. Defining Your Edges

Your edges are the catalysts for your actions. They are your means of strengthening your Umami Vision. They are the core of each of your projects and they need to be reflected in every customer-facing decision you make. They are your way to break the status quo and become innovative. It is good to choose edges that are contrary to the way your competitors run their business (you will validate that with the next exercise).

How many edges should you choose? Two core edges are easy for everyone in your organisation to remember. You might call them extremes. Next to these two core edges you might consider selecting up to three supporting edges: they are not as crucial as your main two but they help you to deliver more nuanced experiences (in other words, they add the extra spice to your projects).

| GOAL: Select and define your differentiators.

1. Gather your team and bring a large selection of customer quotes gathered through your Umami Baseline.

2. Read these quotes individually.

3. Ask everybody to write at least three future customer quotes (quotes you would like your customers to be saying about your brand in one year's time). At least one of these quotes should touch upon your Umami Vision. The remaining quotes can talk about more imme-diate interactions with your brand. As least one of them should address one of the motivators.

4. Together with your team, categorise the quotes, looking for the expe-rience qualities that link them. Name these qualities using adjec-tives (remember to store the results for the following exercises).

5. Choose one quality that reflects one motivator and one that addresses one of the basics. These will become your core edges, your extremes.

6. If you decide to select three supporting qualities, make sure that at least two of them are addressing the motivators. In this way you make sure that you are creating a foundation for designing memorable experiences rather than focusing on fixing the bottom line.

examples of edges that could reflect MOTIVATORS:

Empathy   # Fun   # Engagement   # Meaning

Empathy	Fun	Engagement	Meaning
relaxing	playful	cooperative	proactive
generous	fresh	open	central
informal	virtual	social	inspirational
emotional	unusual	absorbing	diverse
patient	peripheral	discreet	adventurous
warm	implicit	magical	stimulating

examples of edges that could reflect BASICS:

Functionality   # Reliability   # Usability   # Aesthetics

Functionality	Reliability	Usability	Aesthetics
flexible	serious	consistent	creative
new	quiet	intuitive	innovative
formal	unique	time-saving	diverse
personal	durable	uninstrusive	modern
familiar	instant	effortless	colourful
fast	interoperable	daily	striking

6. Benchmarking Your Edges

Your edges are your choice. But it would be advisable to avoid investing in those qualities your competition is already excelling at. Actually, sometimes the smart move might be to use the opposite quality as your differentiator. If, for example, your competitors are being serious and professional, you might consider standing out by choosing playfulness as your differentiator. So, before you commit to your edges, validate them against your main competitors. You can run this exercise on a yearly basis (or whenever a new competitor appears in the market) to check whether your edges are still working for you. If you notice that some of your edges are also addressed by the market, it might be time to choose new ones.

| GOAL: Assess your differentiators against the competition.

1. Choose the qualities you can leverage to distinguish yourself on the market. Select six qualities by which you would like to differentiate yourself on the market. Or maybe you already do?

2. List three of your biggest competitors.

3. Write them down in the corners of the "web".

4. On the scale extending from the middle of the web mark, to what extent are you already developing or demonstrating these qualities? (0 – not at all, 5 – highly). Mark the points and then connect the dots so that a visual graph is created.

5. Mark your competition in the same way (using different colours). Now you can see how you appear in comparison to others. Consider which qualities truly differentiate you, which you should strengthen and which are in no way your unique differentiators.

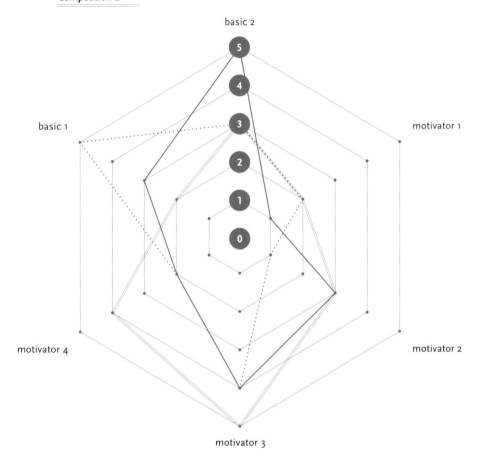

You

Competition 1

Competition 2

7. Resolving Dilemmas

Following a vision and edges comes with a number of choices you have to face: your business dilemmas. Identifying and addressing these dilemmas will help you define a set of principles that will guide your organisation in future decision-making processes.

| GOAL: Defining your strategic principles.

1. Gather as a team. Ask everyone to individually list at least 10 business dilemmas you are going to face when you follow your Umami Vision and your edges. These dilemmas should reflect choices regarding your product, brand positioning, your pricing and any other aspects that relate to your business strategy. Write the extreme choices on the two sides of each line (even if your preference is somewhere in the middle).

2. Present your dilemmas to each other and vote on up to 12 most important dilemmas for your business in the coming months. They could look like these:

Business clients	Individual clients
Premium	Affordable
Stationary	Mobile
Narrow product offering	Broad product offering
Time to market	Quality first
Ecosystem	Independent products

3. Ask every team member to mark with their initials where they see you should be with respect to each of these dilemmas.

4. Once everybody has written their initials, open up a discussion regarding each dilemma. Start by discussing the aspects you seem to agree on. Based on what you discuss, write down a list of three DOs and three DON'Ts (per dilemma) that reflect your agreements.

5. After you have discussed the choices you are aligned on, move on to discussing those where there is more discrepancy. Start by asking people with the most extreme views to give their arguments first. So, for example, in the case of the dilemma: Premium — Affordable, ask AS and JH to state their arguments and then open the floor for a more general discussion. Come to a common understanding and an agreement written down as your list of three DOs and DON'Ts.

   It is recommended to limit the time for discussion about each dilemma as these discussions have a tendency to be very long. Try to dedicate 30–45 minutes to discussing each dilemma where you seem to be in agreement, and 60–90 minutes for those that are more controversial.

6. Based on all DOs and DON'Ts you come up with, define a list of principles for your business strategy: the high-level guiding heuristics to help you set the boundaries to your actions, outputs and outcomes.

8. Defining Umami Metrics

In his seminars, Douglas Hubbard, author of *How to Measure Anything*, often asks his audience to present him with a possibly immeasurable challenge. These challenges are often things such as "mentorship", "love", "trust" or "experience". What Douglas then asks is, "What do you mean by it (trust, love, etc.)?" The typical response is, "I don't think I know". A similar situation frequently happens with your vision or edges. Once you figure out what you mean by them, things became more concrete and therefore more actionable and measurable.

> GOAL: Define how to measure progress towards your umami vision and edges.

1. Gather your team. Bring the ideal future quotes you generated when you were defining your edges.

2. Choose one or two quotes that best represent your vision. Then choose at least one quote that represents each of your edges. These quotes form your Umami Metrics.

3. Think of any other measure that is important for your organisation: business measures, technological measures, etc. Add them below your Umami Metrics. In this way you have a set of metrics that reflects the goals of your organisation.

UMAMI METRICS (more stories like this)

....

"Using InPost feels like having your packages teleport to the place you want to."
(a type of story representing the company vision)

....

"There is no more efficient way to send and receive my package."
(a type of story representing the extreme efficiency)

....

"I love to receive messages from InPost. They always make me smile."
(a type of story representing the extreme cuteness)

BUSINESS METRICS

....

EBIDTA

....

Growth of customer base

....

Implementation cost

....

...

9. Prioritising with the Umami Table

Building a reputation as an outstanding brand will happen only if you keep on delivering the right results. If you are to do this, you need to carefully select the most important things to focus on as early as possible. The only way to stay focused is to use metrics to aid you in selecting the optimal course of action to meet your goals quicker and more efficiently. Your Umami Table is, in fact, a tool for evaluating your initiatives and making the best decision. There is one additional advantage to it. It helps you manage your intuition. As I have previously mentioned (following the work of Daniel Kahneman), our individual intuitive judgment is not very good. So, you can see the Umami Table as an aid against that bias. It gives you the opportunity to look at each initiative through a different lens and also inform your intuitive judgment with the opinions of others.

| GOAL: Decide what is the next most valuable project for you to do.

1. Gather your decision-making team.

2. List all the initiatives you are considering (you can do this on the strategic level and on the operational level as well, to enable you to compare initiatives of very different sizes). Your metrics form the rows of your Umami Table and your initiatives are its columns. Every initiative can have a negative, positive or neutral impact on each individual metric. In the example of the Umami Table, you can see here I've marked the negative impact using up to three minuses and up to three plusses for positive impact but you can use any relative scoring system that works for you.

		initiative 1	initiative 2	initiative 3
UMAMI METRICS	"Using InPost feels like having your packages teleport to the place you want to." (a type of story representing the company vision)	+ +	+	+ + +
	"There is no more efficient way to send and receive my package." (a type of story representing the extreme efficiency)	+ +	+	+ + +
	"I love to receive messages from InPost. They always make me smile." (a type of story representing the extreme cuteness)	0	+ + +	+
	IMPACT OF EXPERIENCE	4	5	7
BUSINESS METRICS	EBIDTA	+	+	+ +
	Growth of customer base	+	+ +	+ + +
	BUSINESS VALUE	2	3	5
	IMPLEMENTATION COST	70 000	115 000	250 000
	Return on Investment (the sum of experience impact and business value divided by the implementation cost)	9	7	5

3. Take the initiative and discuss its impact on each metric by comparing that initiative to the onset of other scores. Remember to analyse each one of them through the lens of each metric before deciding on the final score. In this way you will delay and inform your intuition. The only exception relates to any initiative that directly harms your Umami Vision, which should be removed. It is like a hard stop.

4. At the end of the analysis, estimate the cost of carrying it out. Write this number in the row below your last metric.

5. Repeat this exercise with all initiatives you are considering before calculating the final score for each of them. In this way you will further delay your judgment. Time your discussion (I suggest spending 30–45 minutes discussing each initiative) or run this exercise in break-out groups.

6. After you have analysed all initiatives, calculate their Return On Investment (ROI). Sum up all plusses and minuses into one number. Then divide that number by the implementation cost. You might end up with a small number so just multiply it by e.g. 10000 to get a natural number.

7. The initiatives with the highest scores should become your top priorities. So, by the end of this exercise you should have a prioritised list of initiatives that bring the biggest value for your customers and your business at this moment in time.

"I must not fear.
Fear is the mind-killer.
Fear is the little-death that brings total obliteration.
I will face my fear.
I will permit it to pass over me and through me.
And when it has gone past I will turn
the inner eye to see its path.
Where the fear has gone there will be
nothing. Only I will remain."

Frank Herbert
Dune

PART III

Keeping the Umami Mindset

UMAMI MINDSET

Umami Vision

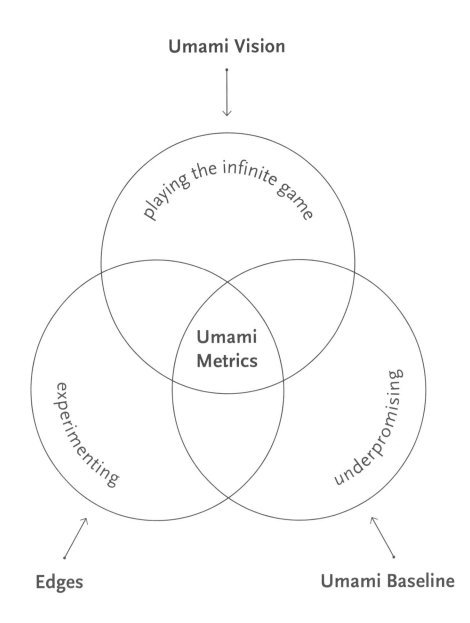

playing the infinite game

Umami
Metrics

experimenting

underpromising

Edges

Umami Baseline

CHAPTER ONE
Positive Adaptation

This could be the end of this book if it weren't for one more human trait, known as "positive adaptation".★ Positive adaptation is usually mentioned in the context of trauma and building resilience (in other words, bouncing back from a difficult situation) but its mechanics are equally applicable in a business context. This is how it works: when we experience a positive change for the first time, we react with a high emotional arousal. We are delighted to take the first sip of our favourite coffee, happy to drive a new car, excited on the first day of our vacation. But over time, these things become a new normal and the initial positive emotion decreases to the point where you take it for granted.★★ This process can be observed in relation to all kinds of aspects of our lives, including winning the lottery, getting a pay rise, changing jobs, possessing products, using services and living through experiences.[171,172,173]

As customers continuously shift their expectations upward, they need to get more and more in order to feel satisfied.[174] Although the intensity of positive emotions always flattens, it happens particularly quickly with respect to material circumstances, like getting a new pair of shoes or a new technological gadget.[175] In other words, we quickly get used to living in material affluence.[176] However, when we are offered experiences, we sustain positive emotions for longer.[177] We also feel that money spent on experiences is more worthwhile, compared with purchasing products or services.[178] But whatever we

★   In scientific literature, this phenomenon is called hedonic adaptation, but the word "positive" seems to be more fitting here.
★★   This is why the first impression is not as important as so many companies think, which I have already mentioned in Part I.

consume, our perception of pleasure and satisfaction with it eventually decreases. For these reasons, positive adaptation is a trying phenomenon for any business.

Why do we adapt?

Imagine yourself going to a doctor. Instead of waiting in line, seated on an uncomfortable chair, the door is opened by a butler, holding your favourite beverage in hand. You are invited into the doctor's office right away, where they await you with a big smile, cookies and a free spa ticket as a farewell gift. They already know that you came down with the flu from having seen your Facebook update, and they have the plan for your treatment ready. Wouldn't you be delighted? What would happen though if you visited that doctor the next time? You would expect to have things happen at least the same way. Perhaps you would even anticipate another little delight on top. Anything else would be a disappointment.

During the first visit, you were delighted because your brain didn't have a pattern anticipating an event like this in its store. The second time you arrived for an appointment, the pattern had already been formed, so you had a baseline ready to compare this new visit to. It might sound disheartening, I know. Remember how our brains are like statistical machines? All experiences we go through are filtered by our senses and then delivered to the brain for interpretation. Any experience thus creates a template through which new input is filtered. In other words, we create a pattern for similar future experiences, and therefore we are eventually less sensitive to them.

Why do we adapt? When we experience high levels of emotions, we tend to stay focused on those intense feelings.[179] This attention can make it difficult for us to function as it takes our attention away from our basic needs. So, we adapt to whatever feelings we experience (both positive and negative) as a means of reducing arousal, allowing us to direct our attention to other needs, as well as new opportunities or threats. A similar process happens with products and services. Imagine that this is the first time you hear about Zappos's 365-day free return policy. It sounds almost too good to be true. But once you try it out, it becomes your new normal. What's more, you begin to expect a similar service from other providers as well. In this way, adaptation becomes your tool for making sense of what's going on around you. It makes you start expecting a similar level of treatment from all services that are being offered to you.

Is there a way to avoid this? Companies might attempt to keep on trying to sustain positive emotions by adding more and more elements that aim at momentary delight for their customers (the so called "wow" effect).★ But as you can easily imagine, this is not the most economical approach. You might end up spending an infinite amount of money piling up new "wow" effects as your customers will keep getting used to them over time. An alternative is to randomly alter the "normal" level of service with the "delightful" level. Each time you visit your doctor you are either treated in a regular way, with the line and no coffee; or in a "wowing" way with butler, cookies and spa tickets. However, as much as it sounds reasonable from a psychological perspective, I am not convinced that many companies would dare to do it. Is there another way then?

Slowing down positive adaptation

I am sorry to say that positive adaptation can't be stopped. But, fortunately, it can be significantly slowed down. The best way to do so is to create an ambitious, inspirational vision for your organisation that gives your customers a sense that they are contributing to a great

★   *Cambridge Dictionary* explains "wow" effect (or "wow" factor) as a quality or feature of something that makes people feel great excitement or admiration. In business, such an effect means a moment of wonder that your client will remember. The "wow" effect is small gestures, attention to client-specific details, or any other action that may make your client feel important and that goes beyond their expectations. The earlier mentioned Kano Model calls these wow effects satisfiers – the surprise elements customers don't even know they want but are delighted with when they find them. The Kano model, however, misses out on understanding the extent to which positive adaptation impacts satisfaction from such features.

cause (which, in turn, offers them personal meaning). Actually, if you truly want to battle positive adaptation, this is the most promising strategy as it is based on invoking a feeling of deep appreciation in your customers towards your cause, rather than only toward the products or services you offer them.

I have already talked about Patagonia but let's look deeper into how they translate their vision into action.[180] Its founder, Yvon Chouinard, is an arduous climber. In 1970, on a winter climbing trip in Scotland, Chouinard impulsively purchased a rugby shirt. Built to withstand a rugby match, it withstood the climb equally well. Yvon brought a few such jerseys back home and incidentally started a new fashion trend for climbers. To keep up with growing demand his team ordered such jerseys first from England and then from New Zealand and Argentina. They all sold out. By 1972, Chouinard was selling not only jerseys but also lightweight waterproof jackets and sleeping bags from Scotland, boiled-wool gloves from Austria and hand-knit reversible hats from Boulder. In 1973, Patagonia was born. In this way, Chouinard entered the clothing industry — one of the most environmentally-unfriendly industries on earth.

Did you know that the amount of clothes bought by people in Europe has increased by 40 percent in the last few decades? Clothing accounts for between two and 10 percent of the environmental impact of world consumption as the production of raw materials requires enormous amounts of water and chemicals, including pesticides. Next comes the impact of washing, drying and ironing. Less than half of used clothes are collected for reuse or recycling, and only one percent are turned into new clothes.[181] And then there is the huge impact of the most popular fabric today: polyester. When polyester garments are washed in domestic washing machines, they shed microfibres. These microfibres are tiny and can easily pass through sewage and wastewater treatment plants into our waterways. Unfortunately, they don't biodegrade but float in the waters where small creatures like plankton eat them. In this way polyester makes its way up the food chain back on to our plates.[182] These are only a few of the problems the clothing industry causes our planet.

But from its early days, Patagonia was devoted to protecting the environment.[183] In 1986, it committed to donating 10 percent of yearly profits to small groups working to save or restore the local habitat.* Next, Patagonia started working on reducing its impact as a corporate polluter. They introduced recycled-content paper for their catalogues in the mid-1980s. They worked to develop recycled polyester for use in their fleece. Patagonia's distribution centre in Reno achieved a 60 percent reduction in energy use through solar-tracking skylights and radiant heating. They used recycled content for everything, from the carpets to the partitions between urinals. The existing stores and build-outs for new ones became increasingly environmentally friendly. Furthermore, Patagonia assessed the dyes it used and eliminated colours that required the use of toxic metals and sulphides and then, since the early 1990s, they have made environmental responsibility a key element of everyone's job.

Patagonia is about great products, of course. But what drives their efforts is a vision about saving the environment. If you are a customer of Patagonia's products, it is hard not to appreciate their consistent efforts to save endangered habitats in South America. This is how, by consistently following their vision, Patagonia has been able to slow down positive adaptation over time.

Your edges can also be a means to slow the adaptation process through triggering positive emotions. Consider Monzo — the digital UK bank, popular with millennials, one of the children of YCombinator. Apart from offering the more traditional banking services, Monzo also helps you to manage your money, rather than just spend it. In a way, it aspires to become your personal trainer when it comes to your financial health. Furthermore, it created a democratic culture that extended to its customers, who are encouraged to share suggestions on an online forum for new features they would like. Their efforts to build extreme engagement are motivated by one driving factor: to develop and perfect a product that people will

---

★   They later upped the ante to one percent of sales, or ten percent of profits, whichever was greater.

want, love and recommend to others. By being edgy, Monzo created a strong bond with its customers, which led to referrals accounting for 80 percent of the company's new business.[184] This is an example of using edges to successfully mitigate positive adaptation. But it will only work if you dare to be radically different, if you continue making your customers realise over and over again that their experience with you is better than what your heterogeneously homogenous competition offers.

There is one more way to battle the adaptation process. You could keep on altering which activities your customers take up as well as induce them to perform similar activities in different ways. It is like going to fitness training. You don't want to do the same exercises over and over again in the exact same way. Having a varied offering is what makes you get yourself up off the couch. Who in the business world does this? Probably the best example is Disney. The company doesn't only make animated movies, but it mines all stories through their parks, games and merchandise. Their main product (the movies) serves as a baseline that can be leveraged through the different aspects of the brand.

You might be asking yourself, why bother, if customers are eventually going to get used to anything you offer? There is one crucial reason for it. Positive adaptation is a mechanism to help keep your brand relevant over time. It is your ultimate propeller for action, a trigger for innovation and progress. It will forever challenge you and force you to keep improving. You just need to know it exists and you need to monitor it through your Umami Baseline. You also need to see your Umami Strategy as an infinite game, experiment to find new ways to reach your goals and keep on underpromising. We will look into these three aspects in the final chapters of this book.

CHAPTER TWO
The Infinite Game

Back in 1798, Poland was removed from the map of Europe. My country was split between Russia, Prussia and Austria-Hungary. The popular sentiment was that the Polish culture needed to be eradicated. Yet, the Poles kept on fighting. There was the Kościuszko Uprising and the October Uprising—both failed. And then the Cracow Uprising and the January Uprising—also failed. Finally, the Greater Uprising at the end of WWI managed to impact the provisions of the Treaty of Versailles, granting a reconstitution of the Second Polish Republic.

At that time, the Sultan of the Ottoman Empire had a tradition of inviting the ambassadors of all European countries for a yearly audience. And every year, as the herald called the Polish ambassador, the answer was always the same, "He hasn't arrived, yet." The Sultan knew that Poles were in the infinite game of battling for their independence and that a day would come when it would be regained. This game wasn't about conquering other countries. It was about regaining and then maintaining national freedom. The Poles fighting in these uprisings knew they most likely wouldn't live to see their country become independent but they also knew they were contributing to something bigger than them. That they were building value spanning beyond their lifetime. In game theory such a game is called the "infinite game".[185]

The finite game
The finite game is like any sport—you have a number of known opponents who act according to the rules of the game and at the end of it there is a winner.[186] If you look at any business chasing after the quarterly results or trying to become number one, what game do you think they are playing? It is reasonable to assume that they see

themselves as players in a finite game, a game that ends every quarter or every year and then is resumed again.

A finite game is often fostered by a phenomenon called the "profitability paradox", driving a great number of companies that somehow miss the point that obtaining profit means nothing without building a competitive advantage. Companies that chase opportunities in the name of profitability often find themselves unable to compete successfully while others somehow build a consistent profit in tough industries with thin margins (think of Southwest Airlines as an example here). It is because true profitability is about more than just making money. Such focus on profitability is what Umair Haque, author of *The New Capitalist Manifesto,* calls "thin value".[187] Thin value might generate profit for a while, but it is merely a transfer of money from one entity to another, like telecom companies that charge a service activation cost. It is essentially an unjustified charge as there is no real action behind it. It creates value for business, but only by taking it from the customer. Haque argues that, "We're seeing the endgame of a global economy built to create thin value: collapse. Why? Simple: thin value is a mirage—and like all mirages, it ultimately evaporates."[188]

Rankings represent a finite game. As you follow the arbitrary rules created by someone else that are the same for everyone, you make your experience like the experience offered by everybody else (which is nothing less than triggering the market averaging syndrome). Naturally, rankings help to set the industry standards, but at the same time, they make the experiences indistinguishable across the market. They help you keep on improving the basics, but they also prevent you from becoming remarkable.

Another syndrome of the finite game is the attitude that can be summed up in the phrase: "not on my watch." It basically means that a company is more interested in maintaining the *status quo* for its own gain rather than innovating for the good of the game itself. Kodak is probably the best-known case of such thinking. They were the first to come up with digital photography as early as the 1970s. But, instead of disrupting the market they were ruling at the time, the company

2. The Infinite Game   167

chose to sit on their invention so that they could benefit from their current business. They did so until Fuji introduced digital cameras to the mass market, which eventually led to Kodak's bankruptcy in 2008. A similar story can be told about the music industry, trying everything to stop the popularisation of Napster, and about Hollywood closing its eyes to Netflix and hoping that it wouldn't affect the traditional movie business. As all these examples show, such a strategy might work for a while but there will eventually come a point in time that it won't. There will be a new player, a new kid on the block, that will question the present *status quo* and propose a solution that will supersede it.

Endangering the apex predator

Before Zappos, nobody imagined you could have a whole year to return an item that you bought online. Today, customers get disappointed and might even decide not to shop with you if you don't have a reasonable free-return policy. Before Apple, the quality of packaging might have been a thing in the luxury cosmetics business but not so much anywhere else. Today, customers expect to have the product they purchase wrapped in a way that increasingly resembles gift-wrapping, rather than simply protecting the product. Before Revolut, customers had to have dedicated accounts for different currencies and they were grumpily agreeing to the extra charges for conversion. Today, more and more of them won't even think of using traditional banking services for that anymore. In every case, the rules of the game have changed based on the actions performed by a player many companies in these areas didn't quite expect to see.

I will digress for a moment and introduce two more concepts here. Back in 1991, an organisational theorist, Geoffrey A. Moore, wrote his influential book *Crossing the Chasm*.[189] In it, he explored how diffusion of technological innovation happens and proposed that there was a breach between adopting new technology by the technological enthusiasts, and then by the pragmatic early majority of customers. Moore argued that early adopters have radically different expectations and are motivated by other things than the more traditional buyers, and that addressing these traditional buyers' needs helps a company cross the chasm of wide product adoption in the market. His theory triggered thousands of companies to focus on addressing the explicit needs expressed by an "average customer" who is supposed to be representative of an early and late majority. And once again, a market averaging syndrome was triggered. As I mentioned in Part II, the average customer is looking for familiar solutions, so their input regarding the possible space for differentiation is not very useful. On the other hand, addressing the needs of your ultimate customers can help you stay sensitive to the signals of change in the customer needs that are likely to trigger your innovative thinking and help you stay ahead of your competition.

There is one more concept I would like to explore: the S-Curve. S-Curve is a mathematical function with a characteristic "S"–shaped curve. In business it typically represents the process of growth of company sales or brand popularity, from being niche, through to a rapid, exponential increase in popularity, followed by a tapering or levelling off. The tapering occurs when the number of new customers declines. At this point, growth is slow and only sustained by existing customers who continue to purchase from your brand.[190]

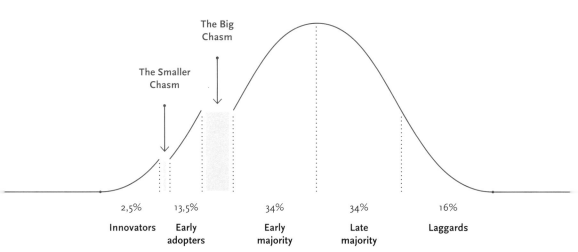

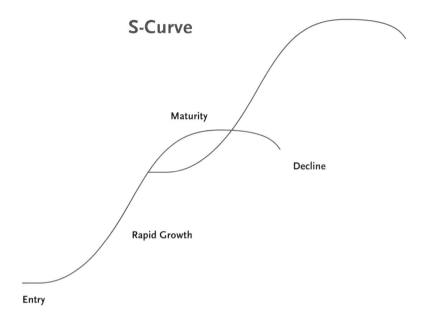

Every business on the planet goes through the S-Curve: they enter the market, then they hit the chasm. If they survive, they experience rapid growth until they hit maturity and eventually decline. Dave Snowden, the founder and Chief Scientific Officer of Cognitive Edge Institute, combined the chasm variation proposed by Moore with the S-Curve model into something he called the "flexuous curve" (or the F-Curve for short).[191] What Snowden realised was that the chasm could be explained by the dominance of one player on the market, one he calls an "apex-predator". Once the apex-predator becomes convinced they are winning the game, there is an opportunity for a new kid on the block to overtake it, change the rules and go for another round of rapid growth. If the new competitor wins, they become the new apex-predator. When the previous apex-predator plays the finite game of creating the ultimate value for their stakeholders, they might be gone, but the game itself goes on. Think of Yahoo being overtaken by Google, or about Spotify effectively overtaking the CD production business. These are examples of how you can become vulnerable to market shifts if you choose to play the finite game.

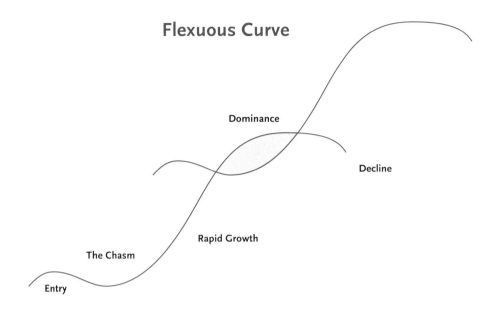

Flexuous Curve

Dominance

Decline

Rapid Growth

The Chasm

Entry

The infinite game

Skiing wasn't always a sport or a recreational activity. For centuries is was solely considered to be a means of transportation. It is said that the Sami (Lapps) were its inventors, and their use of skis for hunting was renowned even in Roman times. But only after the first national skiing competition was organised in Norway back in 1868, did the new era of skiing enthusiasm begin.

Encyclopaedia Brittanica says that before the mid-19th century, skiing was limited by the primitive leather bindings that attached the ski to the boot at the toe.[192] According to tradition (although now subject to debate), about 1860 a Norwegian, Sondre Nordheim, tied wet birch roots from the toes to the heels of his boots to anchor them to the skis. After drying out, the roots provided better stability than leather straps, making downhill skiing possible. As early as the 19th century, Norwegians had designed skis with sides that curved up to form parabolic profiles. Such skis began to be widely used in the 1990s. Along with the technological revolution in how the skis were constructed, it looked like nothing could impact their popularity as the winter activity.

Though origins of snowboarding are sketchy, it is agreed that the first prototype was built in 1965 by Sherman Poppen, an engineer from Muskegon, Michigan. The board was named "Snurfer" by Poppen's wife, who combined the two words that described its purpose: surfing and snow. The initial model was built out of two skis bolted together with a rope attached to the front for steering. Poppen built Snurfer as a toy for his daughters, but its popularity spread, attracting the attention of the Brunswick Corporation, a sports equipment manufacturer, who licensed it and began nationwide production.

The Snurfer's success brought the idea of sliding sideways to a new generation of inventors. The early manufacturers, however, honed their boards in relative isolation. This was until Roger Moore's stunt double used the snowboard for the opening scene in the James Bond movie *A View to a Kill* (1985). From that moment, snowboarding began attracting a whole new group of fans from the skateboarding community.

The grunge- and hip-hop inspired style of clothing of the typical snowboarder couldn't be more different from the traditional ski resort style of those times and that non-traditional aspect was clearly reflected in the title of the first magazine about snowboarding, *Absolutely Radical*, founded in 1985. Despite the initial blowback from the skiing community, snowboarding kept on gaining popularity. Skiing manufacturers had two choices at this point. They could have adopted the finite mindset and tried to "kill" the new sport (and I am guessing that many might have tried to do just that). Or they could choose to play the infinite game and view the introduction of snowboarding as an opportunity for innovation. For example, Rossignol, instead of rejecting snowboarding and the style it brought with it, embraced it in 1987 and adapted their business to create space for this new invention. But it did something further. After expanding into snowboarding and then winter clothing, Rossignol executives thought, "Why can't we become an all year-round sports brand?" They decided to enter the market of bicycles as a way to enable their customers to enjoy the mountains, regardless of the season. Following their vision: "Another Best Day", Rossignol represents an example of an infinite mindset in business.[193]

The infinite game can be characterised by the fact that there are known but also unknown players, rules change over time and the ultimate objective is to keep the game going.★ It is not about winning. It is about outliving your competitors.[194] An organisation with an infinite mindset plays for the good of the game rather than in order to win. You will recognise the organisations who play the infinite game by their ambitious vision, which they live and breathe. These companies focus as much on their own success as they consider their impact on people, community, economy, country and the world. They revel in disruption since they consider it a way to help them transform. They see the new competition as a tool to advance their vision and to sharpen it.

Using the sports metaphor: the finite game would be to aim to run marathons. You could train for it—it would be your finite goal. But you could also see training for the marathon as a way to keep yourself in shape. You could see running the marathon as a motivational tool rather than a goal in itself. Winning every now and then would be a welcome side-effect but not one needed all the time and at any price.[195] If you think in terms of being a player in an infinite game with an infinite time horizon and no finish line, there is no such a thing as winning. In fact, staying healthy (as opposed to curing the symptoms), education (as opposed to getting a diploma), and being a part of a family—these are all examples of infinite games.

Yet, if you look at the majority of businesses, somehow they seem to be stuck in the finite game. If you follow the finite mindset it will quickly push you to want to keep chasing the competition, which will eventually lead to the market averaging syndrome, making you indistinguishable from others. You will keep on chasing the rabbit instead of becoming the rabbit others want to chase. But if you choose to play

★   It is the way children often play. They more often than not play for the sake of playing.

the infinite game, you will find yourself taking radically different strategic decisions from your competition. And maybe not immediately, but the difference will become noticeable over time. Because you will be standing for something. This is why you need your vision and your edges. Without them your organisation will be swayed, if not by this competitor, then by the next. Because there will eventually be someone who will approach the game differently than you and who you will be tempted (but not necessarily able to) to catch up with.

Choosing your game

A bank approached me once with the following challenge. They were using Net Promoter Score (NPS) metrics to measure the performance level in their branches.[196] They set the desired score to 96 (out of 100), which would essentially indicate that, apart from a few exceptions, all customers had to rate the branch experience as excellent. When the results came back, it turned out that all branches across the country scored between 92 and 96. It seemed that their customer service was excellent and nothing needed to change. However, that smelled a little fishy, so I was called upon to propose an alternative.

We followed the Umami steps, and defined the vision for the bank's customer service excellence. They chose the edges, created the success measures and determined how they wanted to verify progress. A year later, I got a phone call. The strategy worked. At that point they had carried out four rounds of validation surveys and they could see that, although the branches, indeed, performed well, there were things to improve upon. Some branches were better at building an emotional connection with customers, some were great with time efficiency and knowledge. But the vision and the edges gave them the infinite purpose to become better and better. Not better than the competition. Better than themselves.

While we worked together, they were struggling with one challenge. A popular business magazine at the time offered a ranking for customer service, which they won for a number of years. But as they adapted the way they served their customers according to their vision and edges, their score went down and another bank took the first position. Their stakeholders started to question the new strategy, so they asked me once again to help them evaluate what happened. We looked into the way the banks were assessed. It was a study, where a mystery shopper came to the different branches and once there, followed a list of arbitrary steps each consultant was supposed to perform. The consultant needed to greet the customer by name. They needed to ask about their well-being before they initiated the transaction, and so on. It was an arbitrary list of customer service standards. Frankly, it was fairly easy to crack. You just needed to mirror that standard and your chances of winning rapidly increased.

My client chose a different route. They wanted to train their consultants for attitude and give them the freedom to execute the service in any way they saw fit. Which effectively meant there was no standard to follow in the first place. And certainly, nobody was following the arbitrary standard the magazine had concocted. As a consequence, they did indeed lose their lead position in that ranking. At the same time, they continued to remain one of the two most recommended financial institutions in the country. Sure, they had to explain to their leaders that scoring highly on that particular ranking (or any other) was not worth changing their practices, when they seemed to be well received by their customers. The edges, the metrics and the customer stories were the tools by which they could argue their case convincingly. They could show that it is far more profitable (in the long run) to be delightfully different than to be exactly the same, even if it cost them that very ranking. And you know what was funny? As the competition noted that customers started expecting a different style of service from their banks, they started to copy the practices of my client.

When you play the infinite game of following your unique Umami Vision, you build an arsenal of experiences for your customers that slow down their tendency to positively adapt to your offering and your brand and you create memories that are word-of-mouth-worthy. Does this mean that you shouldn't study your competition? Not in the least. Your competition reveals your weaknesses. It is, in a way, your sanity check. But if you want to stay consistently different from your competition, you need to keep aligning yourself, your resources

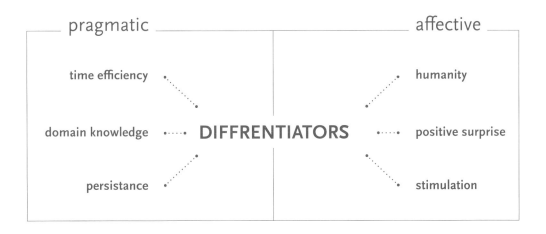

and your decision-making process alongside your Umami Vision. In this way you create a competitive advantage that truly distinguishes you from your competition in a way that is not easily replicated. So, in the deepest sense you become your own biggest competitor. Look at Disney, Tesla, Southwest Airlines, Harley Davidson — they are competing with others only to an extent. But, in fact, they mainly compete with their past selves. Their success is not measured quarterly but in years, if not decades, and it is measured by the impact they evoke. And I bet that once you choose to play the infinite game, you will find yourself ahead more often than you expect. Because this game is about building the long-lasting trust and loyalty of your customers, inspiring them to become better versions of themselves, with you and through you.

CHAPTER THREE
Moving Forward in Times of Complexity

In a letter to a diplomat, dated 1950, President Dwight Eisenhower wrote, "I always remember the observation of a very successful soldier who said, 'Peace-time plans are of no particular value, but peace-time planning is indispensable'." Eisenhower repeated that phrase during a speech in November 1957 in a form that is widely known and used today: "Plans are worthless, but planning is everything." Eisenhower was acknowledging that the act of planning is a process of synthesising and imagining the future, and that the outcomes of that plan do not reflect how things actually unfold. Although he was referring to planning in the context of military action, his observation applies to any planning processes in unpredictable environments.★ And the business world today is nothing if not complex, ambiguous and unpredictable. It is a place where only the infinite game offers a chance to thrive long-term. But along with playing that game, you need to have an effective strategy of quickly adapting your course of action in response to the changes around you and the new information you uncover.

Entering the complex domain
In the influential HBR article "A Leader's Framework for Decision Making", Dave Snowden (the previously mentioned founder and Chief Science Officer of the Cognitive Edge Institute) and Mary E. Boone, a president of Boone Associates, argue that in this complex and unpredictable world, leaders need to develop a new mindset when it comes to decision-making and to acting.[197,198] They propose the Cynefin

★   If the environment is, in principle, predictable but we are not able to make reliable predictions about it and so we have to treat it as unpredictable.

framework as a way of describing the world around us, distinguishing five possible domains in which your business functions.★

The first domain is called the simple or the clear domain. It can be characterised by the premise that the cause and effect relationships between existing patterns are known, linear, empirical in nature and not open to discussion. Think of the procedure that surgeons undergo before entering the operating theatre (dressing up, putting on the mask, washing their hands). This is an example of a repeatable pattern existing in a simple domain, where repetition defines best practice.

The second domain is known as the complicated domain. In this domain, you also find stable cause-and-effect relationships but these relationships are separated over time and space in reaction-chains that are difficult to fully understand. So, they may not be fully known, or they may be known only by a certain group of people. This is where an expert opinion, fact-finding, and scenario-planning are successful tools to execute your business strategy. The practice of traditional engineering, like building bridges, is an example of a discipline in a complicated domain. This is also the domain of any business that functions in the heterogeneously homogenous space.

The third domain of the Cynefin framework is the complex domain. In this domain you can assume that there are cause-and-effect relationships between patterns but you are not able to capture them through analysis as they are influenced and altered by new patterns emerging over time (so there is little stability among them). These patterns can be perceived but not predicted and this is why any technique based on historical data will not prepare you sufficiently to recognise and act upon these unexpected emergent patterns. The complex domain is the domain of any business that aims to stand out in the market. As you aim to differentiate your business, your actions

---

★   "The name Cynefin is a Welsh word whose literal translation into English as habitat or place fails to do it justice. It is more properly understood as the place of our multiple affiliations, the sense that we all, individually and collectively, have many roots, cultural, religious, geographic, tribal, and so forth. We can never be fully aware of the nature of those affiliations, but they profoundly influence what we are."

CYNEFIN FRAMEWORK

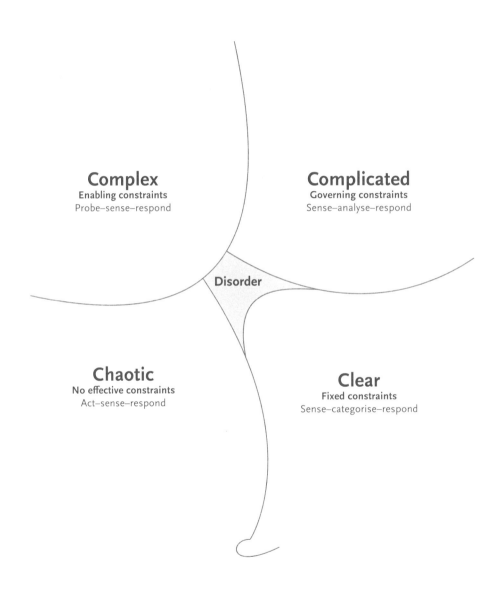

Complex
Enabling constraints
Probe–sense–respond

Complicated
Governing constraints
Sense–analyse–respond

Disorder

Chaotic
No effective constraints
Act–sense–respond

Clear
Fixed constraints
Sense–categorise–respond

will most likely provoke new patterns, which then can be disturbed by the counter-reactions of your competition or new market disturbers.

The fourth domain of the Cynefin framework is called the chaotic domain. In this domain there are no visible relationships between cause and effect and the system itself is unstable. If you find yourself in this domain, you are most likely in some sort of emergency and have the time to react but not to investigate the changes that are taking place. Kurtz and Snowden summarise it in the following words, "The chaotic domain is in a very real sense uncanny, in that there is a potential for order but few can see it — or if they can, they rarely do unless they have the courage to act." If you find yourself in this space the best advice is to act quickly and decisively, to reduce the turbulence, and then to immediately sense how successful your reaction to that intervention was so that you can adapt accordingly. You want to get out of this domain as quickly as possible.

The final, fifth domain, called the domain of disorder, applies when it is unclear which of the other four contexts your business is in. It is the opposite of chaos, as it makes the decision makers think they know what is going on, while, in fact, things happen differently than expected. It is a state of unintentional blindness, where you might not be able to see the coming danger and remain in a state of false comfort. It occurs when people make decisions based on the habitual patterns of their past decision making and avoid failure at all cost. This is probably the most dangerous domain to find yourself in, as it is the space where you may not be able to see new competition growing and endangering your business until they are overtaking parts of your business. Think of mature organisations, stuck in their old ways of doing things — they are examples of entities being in the disorder domain.

Today's market is undoubtedly complex. The sole, most important, characteristic of this space is that you are not going to be able to apply strategies others use, or your own past experiences, to build your success. Relying on benchmarks, historical data or expert opinions may not be sufficient to prepare you to recognise and act upon new, emergent patterns. You might need to discover your own unique approach instead.★ You could achieve this through experimentation within the boundaries defined by your vision and edges.

Why experiment?★★ Because if you experiment, you will trigger different patterns in your customer behaviour, which, in turn, will allow you to "respond by stabilising those [patterns] that we find desirable, destabilising those we do not want, and by seeding the space so that patterns we want are more likely to emerge."[199] Trying things makes all the difference. Only after you start experimenting, will you be able to monitor its impact and adapt your strategy accordingly, increasing your chances for the kind of success that is not easily replicated by others.★★★

Experimentation practice

Why is it so crucial to experiment rather than plan-and-execute? Planning and executing demands that you know from the start where exactly you are going and how you will achieve the intended result. This leads you to only see what you expect to see, which is once again confirmation bias at play.★★★★ Consequently, you fall prey to an assumption that the market situation will be exactly the same when you release your solution as it was when you set out to deliver

---

★   What is important to know about emergent patterns is that they may repeat for a time, but you can't be sure that they will continue to repeat, because their underlying reasons and causal chains can't be isolated.

★★   *Encyclopedia Brittanica* defines experimentation as a "hypothetico-deductive method obtained through direct observation and experimentation and that will, through inference, predict further effects that can then be verified or disproved by empirical evidence derived from other experiments."

★★★ It is worth noting that an experiment that fails may provide more insights than one which succeeds, so you should aim for a percentage of failed experiments as an exercise in stretching your understanding of the emerging patterns around you.

★★★★ I have already mentioned two other situations where confirmation bias is triggered: one when you choose a vision that is a moon shot rather than a Just Cause, and the other when you attempt to make a decision based on a single measure rather than a set of metrics.

Average success rate
of Waterfall projects

Successful	Challenged	Failed
26%	53%	21%

it, which is never the case. You will keep creating offerings that are rooted in the past and remain blind to new patterns.

Until fairly recently, the plan-and-execute approach was the default way of running IT projects. Called a "waterfall approach", it worked like this: you gathered requirements, set the goals, agreed on the approach, got the team together and executed the plan. Sometime later you finished, put your solution on the market and... It has been shown that if your project was of a large scale, the chances of success if you followed the waterfall approach were about nine percent. If the project was small, this rose to 50 percent.[200] Not very promising, right? Imagine such a success ratio when building bridges. Yet, if you look around at various businesses, they seem to ignore the lessons from IT and follow the plan-and-execute approach anyway.

What many of these organisations seem to miss out on is that overcoming geographic obstacles, winning battles or standing out in business are the type of goals best achieved when pursued through experimentation rather than rigid plan execution. This experiment-based mindset can be related to the, sometimes misunderstood, message contained in Richard Dawkins' metaphor of "the selfish gene".[201] Genes that survive the process of selection are those well adapted to their environment. Such adaptation is not the product

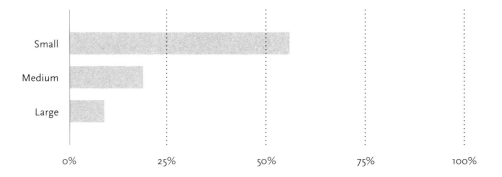

of any intentional design. It is the result of evolution in a universe too complex and unpredictable for any of us to fully understand. Businesses that survive do so because they find ways to adapt to their environment. And that adaptation requires two ingredients: a focus on the greater good of that environment (your Umami Vision) and building on the differentiating characteristics that become the early signals for success or failure (your edges).

The experimentation practice depends on your ability to introduce changes based upon evidence. It is a process of capturing unknown patterns and gradually making them known. Returning to Eisenhower's statement, it is well known to battlefield commanders that the "frictions of war" can rapidly cause the best plans to erode. The same is true of the process of differentiation. There are a great many variables that come into play when trying to form a long-term plan, and certainly too many of them to take into account. So, what is crucial to remember is that any planning is a leap of faith, and ought to be kept as brief as possible. In other words, your experiments must be well defined, safe to fail and designed to help you look at a given situation from different angles. The evidence you gather from experimentation can make results more predictable over time, although we must avoid trying to be predictive. Attempting to predict the future can be grossly misleading as even those of us who are super skilled (and trained) in forecasting are not able to see beyond a six-month horizon.[202] Thus, if you are trying to differentiate yourself from your competition, experimentation is a far more reliable strategy.[203]

Safe to fail

As a complex system has no repeating relationships between cause and effect, it is difficult to assume what is going to work and what is not. But at the same time, it is highly sensitive to small interventions, which is why the best way to figure out what to do next is by experimenting. Snowden proposes the use of "safe-fail probes: small-scale experiments that approach issues from different angles, in small and safe-to-fail ways, the intent of which is to approach issues in small, contained ways to allow emergent possibilities to become more visible."[204] The goal of such probes is not to ensure success but to validate which ideas are useful to follow through with and which should be abandoned. It is counterintuitive in the sense that each such experiment should consist of more ideas that fail than succeed. And for this, it is crucial to increase the organisational tolerance for failure.

Fortunately, there are tried-and-tested techniques for such an approach in the software development world (known under the name of Agile). However, experimentation as modus operandi is still finding its way to the world of business. This is due to the fact that, more often than not, business sees experimentation as a cost rather than an investment. In the finite game of playing catch with competition in the complicated domain, testing alternative approaches seems an unnecessary waste of time, when this time is already scarce. Only after a company consciously decides that their game is the infinite one because it recognises that the playing field is complex rather than complicated, they do become open to experimentation because failure becomes a way to learn rather than a sign of losing the game.

Research through design

There are three important strategic reasons why you need to experiment in order to find how to differentiate your business on the market. Firstly, your customers are not able to verbalise their emotional needs (something that we looked into in Part I), so you need to be able to trigger alternative emotional responses to see which one is desirable.[205] Secondly, they are not able to imagine solutions that don't exist anywhere else, so you need to help them see what you have in mind.[206]

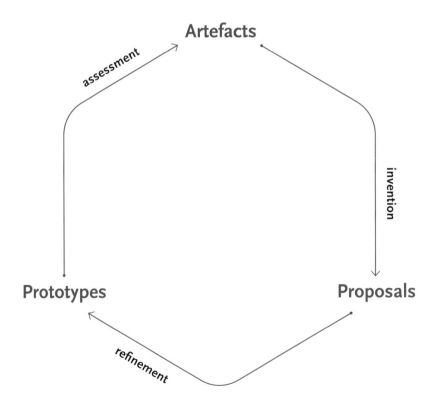

And finally, people are comparative thinkers.[207],★ The ability to make comparisons — to set one object or idea against another and take note of similarities and differences — is the basis of human learning.[208] And since we are used to it from a very early age, we make better judgments when presented with alternatives. This is why traditional business planning and even the design thinking approach are not very successful when applied to the complex domain of business. Fortunately, there is an alternative approach, known as "research through design".[209] In the simplest way, this approach can be explained as "learning by making", and it is based on the following rules:[210]

- you choose situations to explore that, on the one hand, resonate with your vision and your edges, and, on the other hand, have scientific justification (from psychology, neuroscience, behavioural economics or other scientific field related to investigating human behaviour);

- you design interventions that help you to uncover new patterns of human behaviour (this is why it is so crucial to design for your ultimate customer);

- you analyse the results based on systematic reflection through which you capture these new patterns and then translate them into the different design proposals;

- finally, you evaluate these alternative proposals with your customers to see which of them support creation of the patterns you want to emerge and select solutions that best fit your vision and your edges.[211]

★ Comparative thinking already begins when we are infants, trying to identify our mother from among other people.

Let's make it more concrete with an example.★ Some years ago, the telecom company Play, which I have already mentioned, asked me to help them create a unique offering for kids through the research-through-design approach. We tackled this challenge in the following way: firstly, we set out to understand how children of age 6–9 perceive mobile phones. We began by running a series of workshops with children and their parents to see what their perspectives were on mobile phone possession and use. It was fascinating to observe that, contrary to our assumptions, children were in no way interested in any phone "for kids". They all dreamt about a device similar to those their parents (usually their fathers) had. Having an advanced phone was for them a symbol of social status, something which is a crucial aspect of children's development at that age.[212] We further found out that children dreamt of personalising the phone with additional gadgets (covers, stickers, pendants) and that their parents wanted to create a great gift-unwrapping experience for them. Based on our research, we saw the potential of differentiating, not for the mobile phone or even on the mobile plan, but on the packaging and personalisation.

As the next step, we developed a series of packages that reflected the two edges we chose for this project: sustainability and fun. We wanted to design packages that could be reused by children. We started with over 20 concepts, which were then reduced to six that we selected for further testing. One alternative was a hanger for the mobile phone that could be placed above a child's desk. Another was a stand for pens and notebooks with a special holder for the phone. Another would be best described as a "toolbox", with one large compartment and two

★   The Research through Design approach aims to help you better understand not only how people choose and reason about their choices but above all why they make them in the first place. Its goal is to understand the phenomena first before making any design decisions. In this example, I aimed to capture both these functions of Research through Design: understanding *why* kids and their parents are attracted by a certain type of a mobile offering and also *how* to construct an offer that will satisfy them.

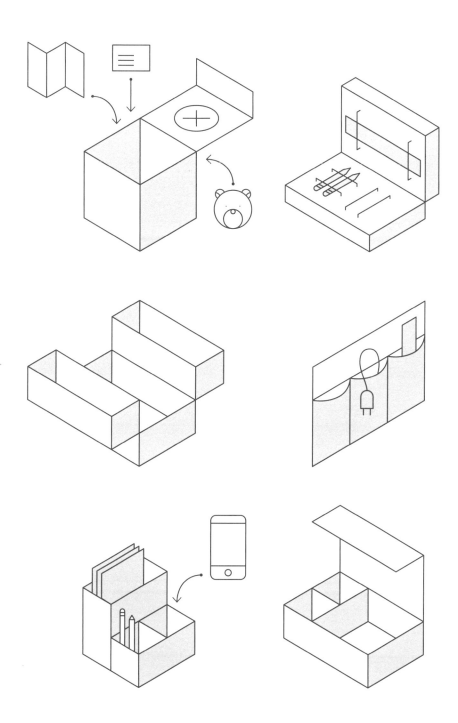

smaller ones. And the last one was something we called a "magic box" — a box filled with a bag, where you could hide different objects.

We then presented these proposals to our future customers. We invited 96 parent-child pairs of participants to something we named "an offer supermarket", which was for us the phase of testing the alternative proposals. Our supermarket included a number of alternative choices regarding the actual mobile plan (like the amount of available internet data, additional applications or games) and the different models of mobile devices with different payment plans. In this way we wanted to understand how parents select the optimal offer for their children and also who made the decisions about each aspect of the offer. Then we gave the kids the option to choose from 60 different gadgets for phone personalisation (they could select three they liked the most) and, finally, we revealed the boxes (each child could choose two of them). The results revealed that the "magic box" and the "toolbox" were the most promising concepts worthy of further exploration.

Finally, we entered the refinement phase. We created the final proposal for the mobile plan and investigated the different visual styles for the boxes. It was fascinating to see that whenever we showed the concept to the customers, we observed a positive emotional reaction to it, from both children and parents. The parents appreciated the ability to manage the internet use the plan construction offered them, and the kids seemed to enjoy receiving a phone and a box filled with personalisation gadgets. This project is an example of a research-through-design approach, rooted in deep understanding of the context and conducted as a series of experiments that allowed us to explore and then redefine the pattern of purchasing the first mobile phone for a child. By the way, it was a big hit.

Research through design is a method for producing new knowledge that is sensitive to human behaviour, preferences and emotional states.[213] In a way, this process follows steps similar to evolution (variation – selection – re-stabilisation) where the proposed transformation is "the result of internally-generated change" with adaptation not triggered by outside forces but by the co-evolution of the different alternatives.[214] In this way, this approach facilitates change towards

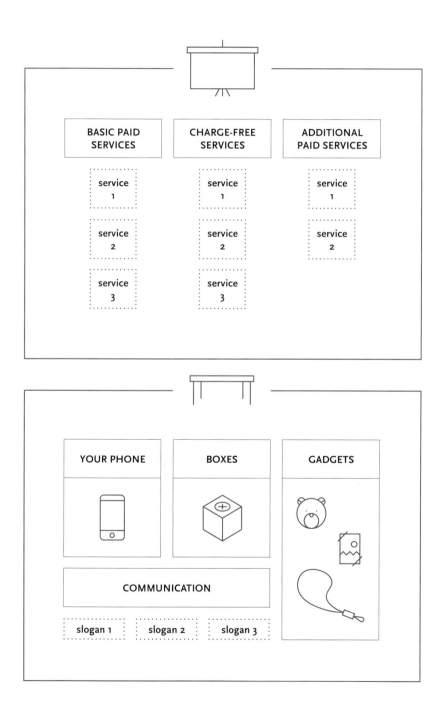

final price: ....

the most efficient outcome while allowing for the safe failure and rejection of other paths. The major advantage of this approach is that it focuses on the change you hope to invoke rather than the improvement of the solution itself. It further offers the possibility of discovering how the various patterns triggered through different propositions could potentially unfold.[215]

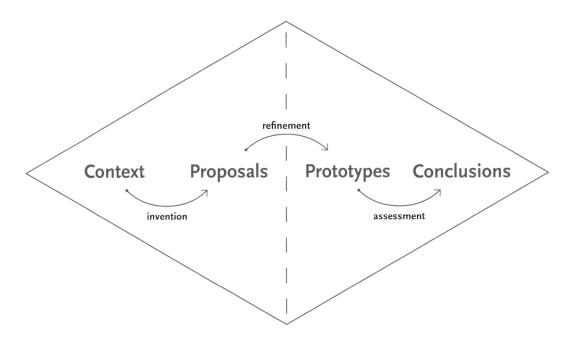

Befriending uncertainty

Paraphrasing Leo Tolstoy, John Kay, the author of *Obliquity*, says, "Unhappy businesses resemble one another, each successful company is successful in its own way. Business achievement depends on doing things that others cannot do – and still find difficult to do even after others have seen the benefits they bring to the imitators."[216] There is a whole lot about the world (including competition and customer behaviour) that we simply can't know. Any business that involves interactions with people is inherently complex and there is no (known thus far) way to figure out the "right" way of doing things that makes you stand out. To achieve your goals requires that you keep learning about them through the process of working out what they are and the only effective way to do this is through experimentation. Experimentation enables you to gain more general knowledge over time that, in turn, helps you make decisions that keep you on your course.

There is another thing worth considering when you set out to execute your strategy. It is best that you stay focused on progress rather than the outcome.[217] This is important because, as you muddle through the uncharted territory of the changing market, you are not going to be able to understand the business and market processes that are happening along the way. So, what you need is an evolutionary approach—one that can be modified through incremental change. President F. D. Roosevelt captured it well by saying, "If high-level objectives are to be achieved, goals and actions need to be constantly revised."

The good news is this: as humans, we instinctively know how to solve daily challenges iteratively and adaptively. We keep on choosing from an unlimited number of options and with limited knowledge at our disposal. Think of taking a new job or buying a house. Different people will make different choices. Not because they don't know what to choose but because there is more than one good option. The same happens to organisations and this is the best opportunity for differentiation, which, in turn, is your best tool to battle positive adaptation. Your path may not be straightforward but it will be an effective one, as it will adapt to the changing conditions of your market and your customers' behaviour while following your vision and edges.

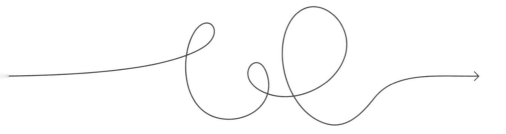

CHAPTER FOUR

The Magic of Underpromising

"After seeing your latest commercial, I hoped you would be better than your competition, but you are the same lying bastard." I keep finding more or less colourful versions of this sentence in the letters and stories of customers disenchanted by brand overpromises. Regardless of the growing knowledge about how disastrous overpromising can be, many companies still think that the only way to get customer attention is to keep on promising more. This attitude is exacerbated as the competition gets fiercer and the money-focused shareholders expect steady 20 percent growth per year. So, in ultimate desperation, many brands are willing to promise anything to get a few more customers through the door. The yoghurt producers tell you that they make the latest best quality yoghurt. The cosmetics companies talk about the improved formula for their soap. The consumer electronics products tease you with the top-of-the-line innovative TV set. And your bank offers you the most competitive offer (that is valid for only a short period of time). But it is not only your bank that promises this. Every other bank has a similar way of tempting customers to switch brand. But, as you see, with similar offers flashed at you from every corner of the street and every corner of the internet, choosing a brand becomes a bit like getting a date through Tinder—just swipe right. And as on Tinder, more often then not you are getting an overly flattering picture which crumbles when faced with reality.

Furthermore, overpromising tends to make your organisation feel like it is playing catch-up. Your employees have only time to do the bare minimum, so they can say, "See, it's technically done." Technically, we have the service we agreed on while signing the terms of agreement. Technically, we have the access to whatever we need unless this is Sunday and the system is down. This rush to keep

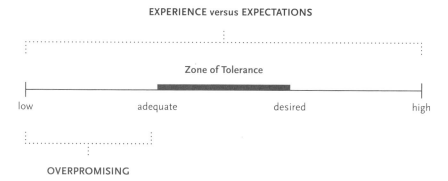

on releasing imperfect solutions to the market likely leads to your employees not being proud with what they produce. So, as well as building a transactional relationship with your customers, you end up developing a transactional relationship with your employees too. It is a relationship that leads to your most talented people leaving whenever a more promising job comes along.

Remember hotels A and B from Part I? In the first case, you were overpromised in the sense that the description of the hotel created expectations that couldn't be realised in the real world. There was no room left for a positive surprise; they could only try to meet your expectations. The problem with such an approach is that the result lands in the space where expectations are higher than the experience itself, making customers feel the adrenaline rush. As a consequence, when you overpromise, you deplete the credibility of your brand and, in fact, trigger your customers to enter a strictly transactional relationship with you, a relationship that will end as soon as a more promising competitor shows up. Because, as Michael Eisner, a former CEO of Disney said, "A brand is a living entity, and it is enriched or undermined cumulatively over time, the product of a thousand small gestures."[218]

Keeping the promise

Promises represent a complex social norm to create obligations, regulate behaviour, reduce uncertainty and build trust. We keep them because they help us to build the foundation necessary for maintaining and evolving relationships. So, in a way a promise is a debt. When a brand makes a promise that something will happen, our brain wants to believe it will. When this promise isn't fulfilled, that consistency that your brain was counting on disappears. It's not only a breach of trust, it is a violation of one of the most fundamental social norms. This goes way beyond disappointment; it alters the way people perceive and interact with your company. A study by Dutch researcher, Manuela Vieth, showed that broken promises cause us to want to punish and seek revenge upon the promise breaker (hence the need to share the negative story with others).[219] Furthermore, such a disappointment overshadows any future interactions between you and the brand. Our brain keeps warning us: "These guys are not reliable, watch out!"

This is why, on the most basic level, customers are drawn to predictability. The root word it descends from is the Latin *praedictus*, which translates as "to foretell". Predictability is about successfully matching customer expectations with the actual experience. It gives your customers a sense of control, increases the feeling of emotional safety and gives a perception of brand reliability. Every fulfilled promise helps you to associate your brand with positivity and trust.[220]

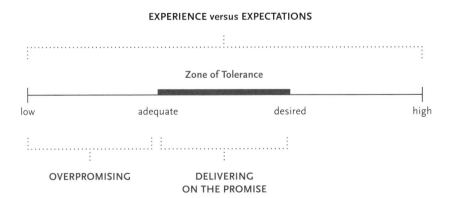

EXPERIENCE versus EXPECTATIONS

Zone of Tolerance

low   adequate   desired   high

OVERPROMISING   DELIVERING
ON THE PROMISE

Yet, if you just deliver what you promised, the brains of your customers will only receive a small shot of dopamine, rendering the experience hardly memorable. While unpredictability caused by overpromising causes stress, in the long run predictability is, unfortunately, seen as unremarkable. It makes us feel like we get the proverbial "bird in the hand." It is good but not too exciting. It is a way to stay in the game but not to stand out.

Underpromising

Think of the following situation. You are having your home repainted. The guy who promises to do it for you declares that it will take two weeks. Three weeks later, the job still isn't finished. How does it make you feel? Probably stressed, annoyed and unhappy. Imagine this situation once more. As the contract promised, the job took exactly two weeks. It is done well but you still need to clean the house afterward to make it liveable again. What do you think? I guess you are satisfied and think it was a job well done but nothing to brag about.

Consider this scenario one last time. After signing the contract, you brace yourself for two weeks of a messy house but the guy is done in just seven days. He has cleaned up after himself, so when you come home you can't spot any sign that there was a construction site there a few hours earlier. How do you feel now? Surprised? Delighted? Happy? And what is the first thing you are inclined to do? You share your story with others. It is no different when it comes to our experiences with brands. We don't only want them to live up to their commitments. We want to be delightfully surprised by them.

A surprise is when our attention is caught by observing an unfamiliar pattern. It acts like a kind of emergency override when our default guessing machine fails and our attention instantly focuses on the unexpected event. If that surprise is positive, customers get a feeling of reward. This is what makes your brand a memory worth remembering and your brand story something worth sharing with others.[221]

Here's one more thing: underpromising gives you the space to experiment and try different courses of action. Underpromising offers the space for mistakes and possible setbacks without incurring the organisational stress which is so typical in situations when you overpromise. Finally, when you underpromise, you are able to surprise not only your customers but often also yourself by going further with what you are able to deliver. It's called positive reinforcement. It works on humans. And it works on organisations.

When talking about underpromising, you might worry that this means setting low expectations. Quite the opposite! Whatever you promise to your customers needs to be on a par with your competition and to build a compelling story about your brand. Otherwise, customers will never consider you in the first place. Imagine a hotel telling you that the comfort of their beds is average and their food is okay-ish. Would you book a night there? Unlikely. But imagine this. You show how great your place is but you don't show all of it. You deliberately create a few hidden gems for your visitors to discover (like a glass of wine waiting for them on the table or a list of local attractions available tonight). Sure, you can let them know they can expect that beforehand in order to catch their attention. But if you choose to miss out some details, there is quite a chance they will be positively surprised. Underpromising is just that—an effective way of managing your customers' expectations and actions to your advantage.

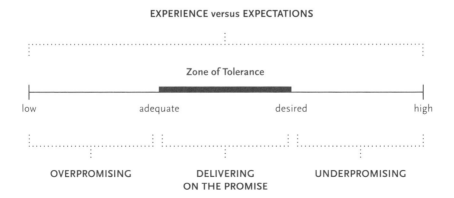

EXPERIENCE versus EXPECTATIONS

Zone of Tolerance

low   adequate   desired   high

OVERPROMISING   DELIVERING ON THE PROMISE   UNDERPROMISING

Steve Jobs was a master of underpromising. He would promise, both to his customers and his investors, more conservative results than expected, and then blow their minds with the actual outcome.[222] Ira Kalb, the president of international consulting and training firm Kalb & Associates, wrote for *Business Insider* that the underpromising strategy Apple used was extremely successful on a number of levels:[223]

1. "It set expectations lower so that the delivered products exceed expectations.

2. It helped to avoid tipping off competitors.

3. It helped to avoid shareholder disappointment and lawsuits.

4. It enabled Apple to gauge any negative reactions to the under-prom-ised products.

5. It allowed the company to respond to these reactions by improving the products before delivery.

6. It generated far more excitement and publicity when the product beat expectations.

7. It quieted detractors who knock Apple and their fans."

The strategy of underpromising is difficult. It demands that your marketing and communications departments consider what they talk about and what they consciously omit. In our current market situation, not shooting all your arrows from your quiver might feel like a mistake. But it is not. Firstly, you might be surprised to realise that the more you advertise, the less your customers are inclined to share their stories about your brand with others.[224] But, once under-promised and then positively surprised, your customers will do your marketing for you. They will tell the stories about your "hidden" fea-tures. And these stories will be much more popular compared with you telling them yourself. In this way, you not only exceed their expec-tations, but you allow your customers to become the multipliers of your marketing and advertisement efforts.[225]

1. It set expectations lower so that the delivered products exceed expectations.

2. It helped to avoid tipping off competitors.

3. It helped to avoid shareholder disappointment and lawsuits.

4. It enabled Apple to gauge any negative reactions to the under-promised products.

5. It allowed the company to respond to these reactions by improving the products before delivery.

6. It generated far more excitement and publicity when the product beat expectations.

7. It quieted detractors who knock Apple and their fans.

CHAPTER FIVE

The Inevitability of Resistance

There is an obvious benefit to standing out in the world where customers are bombarded every day with new opportunities to purchase something. If you are different from your competition, you will be noticed and talked about. And since word of mouth is the ultimate marketing tool of today, it would be crazy not to go after it. Think again of Southwest Airlines, with their policy of hiring remarkable employees to spice up the travel experience. There is little chance you will forget that someone rapped your safety instructions or if they were delivered as a stand-up comedy routine. Yet, despite the obvious viral fame of such examples, not many companies decide to create a remarkable experience for their customers. There is one underlying reason behind this. Standing out is scary.

Meeting resistance

I have spent years helping companies incorporate experience design as their strategic differentiator and I keep on seeing the same pattern. Initiating the first project is not that hard. I am not saying it is easy in the least, but compared to the further stages, it is a proverbial piece of cake. If enough employees within a company are willing to try to design an experience for their customers, a few projects will happen sooner or later.

However, the more advanced the organisation becomes with respect to delivering experiences, the harder it becomes to move forward. This manifests in the form of resistance by the decision makers to change the old ways that used to work, for something new, unknown and potentially risky. I am not saying that decision makers are unable or unwilling to change. But they have many years of experience running their business in a certain manner and it is hard to change these old ways, especially if the old ways have served them well for so long. It is a dance with fear, where the choice is to either do things like we always did, risking that over time, our Return on Investment will diminish, or to try a new approach with the high risk of making mistakes and landing flat on our face if this new strategy doesn't deliver the expected outcomes in a given time-frame. This risk feels even more real when no "proven approach" is available — something that takes an edge off this ocean of strategic uncertainty.

Like individuals, organisations suffer from being afraid. The best description of that fear, otherwise called Resistance (with a capital R), is captured in a little manifesto written by Steven Pressfield called *The War of Art*.[226] Although Pressfield writes about the fear we experience as individuals, his ideas are equally relevant to organisations.

He argues that Resistance is a powerful force that keeps us from reaching our potential, and makes us stay average. It is a force preventing us from following a different path from the line of, well, least resistance.★ Resistance makes us stay focused on short-term goals, instant gratification and immediate pleasure. It loathes long-term thinking, commitment and radical change. It will encourage you to keep on doing more of the same and discourage you from choosing to do something different from the mainstream. In other words, it will push you to follow the market and keep on falling into the trap of becoming heterogeneously homogenous. It will keep on discouraging you from playing the infinite game, experimenting and underpromising. And it will discourage your bosses and peers as well. The more outlier-like thinking your organisation displays, the stronger Resistance will be — if not from the leaders, then from the shareholders and other outside and inside agents that lobby against change. They will do whatever is in their power to keep you on the "safe" track. To make you stay average. Be more of the same. This is why it is so hard to change any organisation.

★   According to *Collins Dictionary*: "If you take the line of least resistance in a situation, you do what is easiest, even though you think that it may not be the right thing to do."

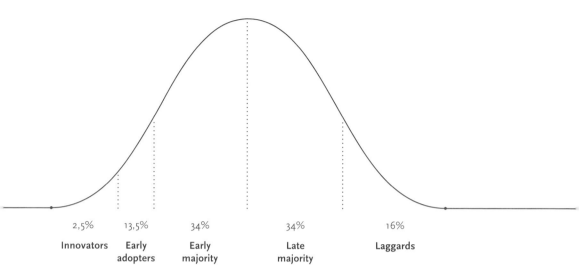

2,5%	13,5%	34%	34%	16%
Innovators	Early adopters	Early majority	Late majority	Laggards

But organisations also follow the Technology Adaptation Curve proposed by G. Moore.★ There will be innovators and early adopters who will want to help you differentiate in the market (and there will be laggers too). And there will be a vast majority sitting on the banks and waiting to see what happens, which is okay as long as you know who is who and find the right people to join your team. You just need to remember that it is not impossible to become different and there are numerous examples to prove it. But like any skill you want to acquire, it requires long-term commitment and effort.

Outlier mindset

If Resistance is so strong, is there any point fighting it? Wouldn't it be better to just give in? This, certainly, is an option. But it is a short-term option, because sooner or later a new competitor will appear that will have more courage to stand out, to create an emotional rather than only a transactional bond with their customers. Most probably it will be a startup that does not share your Resistance — how are you going to compete with them? So, sure, you can keep on doing

★   We could call it the Differentiation Adaptation Curve or the Umami Adaptation Curve.

more of the same, running the risk of eventually losing the game and becoming irrelevant. But what if you don't? There are three ingredients (three Ps, if you like) your organisation needs to cultivate to build the outlier mindset: *purpose, passion* and *patience*.

Purpose is nothing more than consistently and relentlessly executing your vision: this idealistic North Star you set for yourself to follow. You need to have your and your organisation's heart set 100 percent on that vision. And you need to believe that there is a path to reach it. If not that path, then another (this is what your edges are for—to help you choose the path that works in any given moment). Truly believing in your vision will motivate you to keep going and to focus on progress, rather than becoming discouraged that the ultimate goal is far away or treating it as a corporate slogan.

Purpose's best friend is *passion*. Passion makes you ignore the fact that achieving your vision might be hard. The fact that certain things seem impossible falls by the wayside, and you decide to try them anyway. Passion will help you keep experimenting and testing new directions while underpromising results to the market. And the only way to keep the desired level of passion is to not allow yourself to overthink the risks and difficulties you might find on your way. It is like cultivating for yourself the mindset of early explorers like Christopher Columbus or Vasco da Gama: you are preparing yourself to set sail into the unknown hoping to discover new ways of differentiation. Being passionate is, in this sense, not a sign of madness but a sign of open curiosity and the flexibility to accept what happens along on the way.

Once you decide you are going to follow the path of being different, the key is to keep on moving to your own rhythm rather than the rhythm dictated by your competition. And for this you need to be *patient*. Patience is about finding the pleasure in following your own path, consistent with trying new things out. It helps you stay focused on the long term rather than being swayed by short-term objectives and the movement of the current market. It gives you the capacity to tolerate experimentation and failure. If you are impatient, you will have a tendency to make overpromises, ultimatums and deadlines that may or may not be considered reasonable. Impatience is the ultimate self-sabotage. It clouds your judgment, detracts from your credibility, and damages relationships. Patience will aid you in waiting for the right opportunities, accepting challenges ahead and avoiding the "ready, aim, fire" syndrome. It is a way to build the right culture for your vision and to give your employees the time to see that you are serious when it comes to your goals and ambitions. The bottom line is that patience is the appreciation for living an adventure in all its aspects: good, bad and scary. Finally, patience is your ultimate means to survive the dip.

The dip

The dip (otherwise known as the chasm, which I previously mentioned when I talked about the infinite game) is the main reason why so many organisations give up on becoming different. It is the moment when you think that there are too many difficult obstacles in the way of pushing through with your vision and your edges. This is the moment when most companies go back to doing what's safe instead of following the outlier path. Yet, as Seth Godin says, "The dip is the secret to your success. The people who set out to make it through the dip—the people who invest the time and the energy and the effort to power through the dip—are breaking the system because instead of moving to the next thing, instead of doing slightly above average and settling for what they've got, they embrace the challenge."[227] What Godin notices is that when you first start doing something it's fun. You keep on rapidly learning, which helps you to keep going. And then you hit the dip—the long slog between starting and mastery. This is the time to build your unique competitive advantage, not in one brilliant move, but step by step. This is why you need the three P's to help you deal with the dip. They form the foundation for self-trust. Build your flanks against Resistance. Resistance hates purpose and passion. But, above all, it hates patience. Patience makes it win the battles but lose the wars, while purpose and passion are the bullets defending your goal.

You just need to keep your eyes on the prize. If you dare to stand out your reward will be 10 times as big as that of whoever is number two. How come? Did you know that the most favoured ice cream flavour in the world (according to the International Ice Cream Association) is vanilla?[228] It sells almost four times as much as the next beloved flavour, chocolate. This phenomenon happens not only with respect to ice cream flavours, it also happens in business and it's called Zipf's Law. In the 1930s, Harvard linguist George Kingsley Zipf found that "the" (the most used English word) occurred about twice as often as "of" (second place), about three times as often as "and" (third) and so on.[229] But as it turned out, Zipf's Law has much further reaching implications than logging word usage. In much the same way, you can observe this tendency in the size of meteors, hard drive disk errors, frequency of earthquakes and price returns on stocks. And, of course, it also applies to brands.[230] If you are first on the market you will win big. If you are second, you still win but significantly less. And if you are third, fourth, etc. you just get a tiny fraction of the success.

Why is this the case? As humans we want to have a guarantee of success because our brains don't want to waste energy on interactions that wouldn't meet our expectations. If you tear your ligaments, you don't want to go to any old surgeon. You want the best. If you travel to

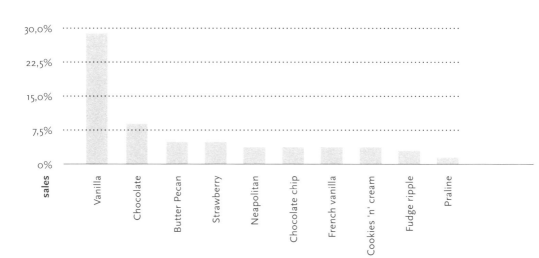

a new place, you want to see something interesting, if not spectacular, not something boring. If you choose a product or a service, a similar sentiment is at play. You dream of choosing your ultimate best option, the option that fits with who you want to be. Sure, if you don't have that option, you will choose from among what's available (this is why so many businesses are still operating) but this relationship will remain transactional. And as soon as a daring outlier enters the market, your customer may not have any qualms about leaving you and switching. And be sure that, sooner or later, this new player will show up. It can be your competition or it can be you. You need to decide.

Start with reflection

Did you notice how often people in different organisations never quite realise why they do what they do? In Poland we have a saying that people keep on running in such a rush with their wheelbarrows that they forget to load them up. Such behaviour is escalated even further at a leadership level. You might find yourself having to make so many decisions and to participate in so many meetings that there is no time and energy left to think — not only about long-term issues but even to consider what should be done next. In this hamster wheel of urgent decision-making it is easy to forget that your focus determines your reality. It gives you a sense of what your priorities are and therefore what the priorities of your employees need to be. The roots of keeping your priorities in focus are hidden in reflection.★

Back in 2006, Judy Sorum Brown, a senior fellow at the University of Maryland's James MacGregor Burns Academy of Leadership, wrote an article about the growing importance of reflection in leadership.[231] She argued that, "The world in which we lead is like an iceberg, with only the tip of it seen above the waterline. That tip is represented by events.

★   Reflective leadership is not a new concept. Back in 1933, the philosopher John Dewey described it as a form of problem solving. He said that reflection "includes [...] the sense of a problem, the observation of conditions, the formation and rational elaboration of a suggested conclusion, and the active experimental testing."

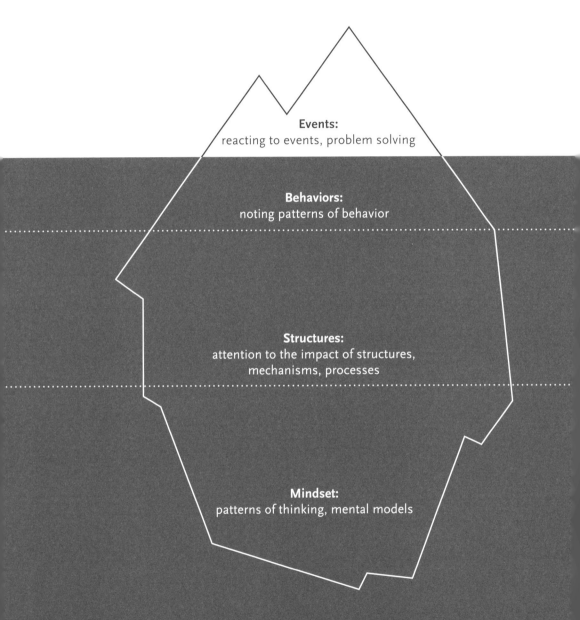

Events:
reacting to events, problem solving

Behaviors:
noting patterns of behavior

Structures:
attention to the impact of structures,
mechanisms, processes

Mindset:
patterns of thinking, mental models

**When mindset changes,
everything above it shifts**

Everyone is watching the tip because it's visible. Yet most of the iceberg, as we all know, is below the waterline. And below the waterline are the dimensions of organisational life that are shaping what we see."

Brown went on to explain that any leader faces events: those anticipated, and those not anticipated. But this is just the tip of the organisational iceberg. Below that you will find the behavioural patterns that dictate your organisational actions. Think of such patterns in your organisation—some behaviours push it in a direction that is joyful and productive, while others probably hamper it. These patterns are, in turn, influenced by the conscious and unconscious organisational structures and rules. And finally, there are mindsets, ways of thinking that create these structures, that produce the patterns that result in your organisational actions. If you hope to truly focus on your vision and your edges you need to aim to transform the mindsets or, in other words, the stories of your employees. These stories determine where your focus lies and how your organisation operates.

Thus, your ability to become an outlier begins with your capacity to explore and change the ways of thinking of your organisation. It doesn't make much sense to tinker on the top with projects and activities, if you are not changing the organisational mindset alongside this. If you make a shift at a lower level of the iceberg, everything will align accordingly. If you are wondering what your first step should be, try a little reflection with the following questions:

- Where does your organisation come from?
  How has your past shaped who you are today?

- What makes you strong and what makes you weak as
  an organisation?

- Who is your competition? What differentiates you from them?

- Why do your customers want to use your offering?
  What makes them reluctant to use it?

- Why do your employees want to work with you? What discourages them?

- What is the reason for you to get out of bed, go to work and stay excited about your organisation day after day? What would be the biggest possible change your organisation could bring to the world?★

The answers to these questions, along with the Umami Baseline, will become the basis for your vision and help you become the outlier you want to be. And if you are committed to changing your organisational culture you might consider looking at the Umami Model from the perspective of your employees. If you tune in to their stories, you will be able to understand not only what your organisational culture is today, but also what you can do to shape it into what you want it to ideally become.

★   You can download a template for the Reflection Journal from
www.agaszostek.com/umami-method

Afterword

In 2012, the stock price of Best Buy sank to 12 dollars a share, the lowest in a decade. The challenge the company faced was a new behaviour called "showrooming". Customers learned to come to the stores to see a product and then buy it online. It would have been a ride down the hill if not for the fact that Best Buy realised it had two things online shops didn't — a place where customers could touch and experience different products, and their famous tech-support service: Geek Squad.[232] The chain decided to rethink what the shopping and installation experience was about, and to move from selling boxed products to becoming an advisory service with the best customer support imaginable. This was a way to monetise on extreme empathy, something that didn't only keep Best Buy afloat but also made it stand out from online platforms. Too bad the company needed a near-death experience to shake their worldview and nudge them to arrive at such a conclusion. Perhaps there is no need for you to wait for such extreme circumstances. In this book you can find a way that shapes a brand your customers not only remember fondly but also want to talk about.

Being different is like entering uncharted territory. So, if you don't feel freaked out at least a little, you are not there yet. On the other hand, if you once dreamed about becoming an explorer setting out for an expedition to the ends of the known world, this is the spirit you need to hold on to. And the best thing is this — maybe not tomorrow, maybe not next quarter, maybe not even next year, but it will be profitable to follow that path. Profitable to a level you can't begin to imagine.

"You're mad.
Bonkers.
Off your head.
I'll tell you
a secret...
All of the best
companies are."

paraphrasing Lewis Carroll

So,
what kind
of outlier
would
you like
to become?

Thanks

It was the final exercise of the AltMBA workshop. I wrote three goals for myself for the following weeks and months to come:

- create tools that support the strategic thinking of experience design;
- run a series of radical design projects; and
- create some sort of educational programme for experience design.

I was evaluating these goals with David Donde, the charismatic owner of the TRUTH Coffee Roasters and Cafe in Cape Town, South Africa (if you are ever around, you must visit his place). David kept on digging, figuring out whether or not I was hiding from what I really wanted to do. At some point he provoked me to say, "I want to do all of this, so that I can write books." There was a long silence as the meaning of the words that burst out of me sank in. Then David smiled broadly and said, "Now, I believe we have just surfaced your true goal."

This conversation made me suddenly remember that I've been dreaming about writing since I was a teenager. While my friends wanted to be actresses and singers, I wanted to be a writer. I have even reported for the local newspaper about high school news. Then my life took a different turn and this dream lay dormant until David woke it up again. David, thank you so much for being so persistent and so generous with me!

It was the very beginning of the process that eventually led to writing this book. In the meantime, I designed a number of tools for designers, I led a radical design team and I co-designed (together with my friends Jericca Cleland, Pim Schabschatel, Beverly Jiang,

Alex Grots and Melanie Dorey) a series of educational workshops advancing the field of experience design. But this book had to be written.

So, first and foremost I would like to thank you for reading this book. I hope it was as inspirational for you to read it as it was for me to write it, and that it offered you a new perspective on how to strategise on the topic of experience design.

The person who is there for me always, is my amazing husband Łukasz. He was the person who read this book line by line checking for inconsistencies, repetitions and any other mistakes I might have accidentally let in. Without him I wouldn't be who I am and this book wouldn't exist. Thank you for being there for me, even when I disappeared inside my head for days. You are the best husband ever!

I would further like to thank Ann Morgan — my amazing, encouraging and provoking mentor. When BIS Publishers kindly agreed to publish this book, I realised that I needed professional support. I contacted the Ruppin Writers Agency seeking a mentor and Ann agreed to help me. Ann, your insights and comments helped me elevate this book to the next level. Without your help, it wouldn't be what it is. I would also like to thank Diane Parker and Scott Sharp, my copyeditors, who turned my Ponglish into beautiful English.

Dominika Wysogląd, Tomek Bierkowski and Agnieszka Gontarz created the visual layer for this book. Dominika, you are the best graphic designer I know and working with you is an ongoing pleasure. I hope there is a long line of joint projects ahead of us. Tomek, you were our amazing book design mentor — your support helped us make this book look the way it does. Thank you! Agnieszka, your patience for all changes was endless. You helped us put this project together and I am grateful for it.

I would very much like to thank BIS Publishers and Bionda Dias for believing in this project and taking the risk of publishing it. I am deeply grateful for your trust. And this is the moment to also thank Ruud Janssen and Roel Frissen, the authors of *Event Design Handbook* who not only encouraged me to write but also recommended me to BIS Publishers. Your friendship means the world to me.

I read the *Experience Economy* by Joe Pine and Jim Gilmore many years ago. I was struck by how insightful and forward-thinking this book was. Back then, few people believed how important experiences would become for business. Twenty years later, here we are in the era of the experience economy. And I remain inspired by the work of Joe, who keeps on deepening the understanding of what experiences mean to business. Joe, thank you for not only inspiring this work but also helping to shape it with your insightful comments and suggestions. You are my mentor and my inspiration.

There is another person who taught me a lot about connecting business with experience design — Jørgen Bang-Jensen, the former CEO of Play Telecom. Jørgen, you made me realise that business was struggling to incorporate thinking about experiences into the traditional way of doing business. Working alongside you was the best business education ever. Thank you for your trust and for your patience with me.

I am also grateful to my early readers — April K.Mills, Piotr Jegier, Dawid Wiener, Anna Pohlmeyer, Darek Kędziora, Katie Zazensky, Pim Schachtschabel, Anthony Rocco, Werner Puchert, Petter Abrahamsen and Ask Agger. Your comments (sometimes really critical) kept on pushing me to level up and go the extra mile to improve this book. Particularily, I would love to express my deepest gratitude to April for gifting me with such a generous and powerful foreword. I had tears in my eyes when I first read it.

Andy Sontag and Katja Wessling from Kaospilot, the alternative business school in Denmark, showed their enthusiasm for the methodology described here — thank you for your trust and encouragement.

Before I sat down to write this book, I was tossing around some of the ideas captured here by writing short articles on Medium. Fabricio Texeira, the founder of the UX Collective, kept on publishing these stories and also agreed to check the early draft of this book and endorse it. Thank you, Fabricio!

Last but not least, I would like to thank my amazing AltMBA friends: Steven Thomas, Alison Esposti and Philip Collins. Having you to watch my journey and encourage my efforts was invaluable. I am so thankful to have you in my life.

Finally, I would like to mention two more influences on my thinking and the Umami Method: Simon Sinek and Seth Godin. My ideas about defining an ambitious purpose are drawn from Sinek's work. My understanding of the notion of the finite and infinite game is also rooted in his writing. Seth has inspired me to think about the concept of the ultimate customer and about edges, and offered me the vocabulary to explain it. Thank you!

Notes

PART I: Discovering the Competitive Advantage of Experiences

CHAPTER ONE: The Experiencing and Remembering Self

1   Van der Merwe, S.E., Biggs, R., Preiser, R., Cunningham, C.,
    Snowden, D.J., O'Brien, K., Jenal, M., Vosloo, M., Blignaut, S.
    and Goh, Z., 2019. Making sense of complexity: Using SenseMaker
    as a research tool. *Systems*, 7(2), p.25.

2   Godin, S., 2009. *Purple Cow, New Edition: Transform Your Business by
    Being Remarkable*. Penguin.

3   Johnson, G., 2016. *Exploring Strategy: Text and Cases*.
    Pearson Education.

4   Hassenzahl, M., 2010. Experience Design: Technology For
    All The Right Reasons. *Synthesis Lectures on Human-Centered
    Informatics*, 3(1), pp.1–95.

5   Kahneman, D. and Riis, J., 2005. Living, and thinking about it:
    Two perspectives on life. *The Science of Well-being*, 1, pp.285–304.

6   https://www.kickstarter.com/projects/martinkallstrom/
    memoto-lifelogging-camera

7   http://getnarrative.com/

8   Gurrin, C., Smeaton, A.F. and Doherty, A.R., 2014. Lifelogging:
    Personal big data. *Foundations and Trends in Information Retrieval*,
    8(1), pp.1–125.

9   Hassenzahl, M., Eckoldt, K., Diefenbach, S., Laschke, M., Len, E.,
    and Kim, J., 2013. Designing moments of meaning and pleasure.
    Experience design and happiness. *International Journal of Design*,
    7(3).

10   Juster, T.F., and Stafford, F.P., 1985. Time, Goods, and Well-Being. *Ann Arbor: The Institute for Social Research*, University of Michigan.

11   Argyle, M., 2003. Causes and correlates of happiness. *Well-being: The Foundations of Hedonic Psychology, 353.*

CHAPTER TWO: The Nature of Expectations

12   Mitchell, T.R., Thompson, L., Peterson, E. and Cronk, R., 1997. Temporal adjustments in the evaluation of events: The "rosy view." *Journal of Experimental Social Psychology, 33*(4), pp.421–448.

13   Wirtz, D., Kruger, J., Scollon, C.N. and Diener, E., 2003. What to do on spring break? The role of predicted, on-line, and remembered experience in future choice. *Psychological Science, 14*(5), pp.520–524.

14   Schkade, D.A. and Kahneman, D., 1998. Does living in California make people happy? A focusing illusion in judgments of life satisfaction. *Psychological Science, 9*(5), pp.340–346.

15   Schwarz, N. and Xu, J., 2011. Why don't we learn from poor choices? The consistency of expectation, choice, and memory clouds the lessons of experience. *Journal of Consumer Psychology, 21*(2), pp.142–145.

16   Gilbert, D.T. and Wilson, T.D., 2007. Prospection: Experiencing the future. *Science, 317*(5843), pp.1351–1354.

17   Csikszentmihalyi, M., 1999. If we are so rich, why aren't we happy? *American Psychologist, 54*(10), p.821.

18   Zeithaml, V.A., Parasuraman, A., Berry, L.L. and Berry, L.L., 1990. *Delivering Quality Service: Balancing Customer Perceptions and Expectations.* Simon and Schuster.

19   Allen, M. and Friston, K.J., 2018. From cognitivism to autopoiesis: towards a computational framework for the embodied mind. *Synthese, 195*(6), pp.2459–2482.

20   Shah, P., Harris, A.J., Bird, G., Catmur, C. and Hahn, U., 2016. A pessimistic view of optimistic belief updating. *Cognitive Psychology, 90,* pp.71–127.

21   Shepperd, J.A., Carroll, P., Grace, J. and Terry, M., 2002. Exploring the causes of comparative optimism. *Psychologica Belgica*, 42(1/2), pp.65–98.

22   Gouveia, S.O. and Clarke, V., 2001. Optimistic bias for negative and positive events. *Health Education*. 101(5), pp. 228–234.

23   Varki, A., 2009. Human uniqueness and the denial of death. *Nature*, 460(7256), p.684.

24   Johnson, D.D. and Fowler, J.H., 2011. The evolution of overconfidence. *Nature*, 477(7364), p.317.

25   Taylor, S.E., 1989. *Positive Illusions: Creative Self-Deception and The Healthy Mind*. Basic Books.

26   Seligman, M.E., 2004. *Authentic Happiness: Using The New Positive Psychology To Realize Your Potential For Lasting Fulfillment*. Simon and Schuster.

27   Seligman, M.E., 2006. *Learned Optimism: How To Change Your Mind and Your Life*. Vintage.

28   Parasuraman, A., Berry, L.L. and Zeithaml, V.A., 1991. Understanding customer expectations of service. *Sloan Management Review*, 32(3), pp. 39–48.

29   McDougall, G.H. and Levesque, T., 2000. Customer satisfaction with services: putting perceived value into the equation. *Journal of Services Marketing*.

CHAPTER THREE: The Experience Equation

30   As referred to in the article by Wilson, M., 20 June, 2011. Survey details importance of a store's external appearance. *CSA*. Retrieved from: https://chainstoreage.com/real-estate/survey-details-importance-stores-external-appearance

31   Kahneman, D., Fredrickson, B.L., Schreiber, C.A. and Redelmeier, D.A., 1993. When more pain is preferred to less: Adding a better end. *Psychological Science*, 4(6), pp.401–405.

32 Kahneman, D., 2018. Daniel Kahneman on misery, memory,
    and our understanding of the mind. *NPR*. Retrieved from:
    www.npr.org/2018/03/12/592986190/daniel-kahneman-on-misery-
    memory-and-our-understanding-of-the-mind?t=1584617416908

33 Kahneman, D., Fredrickson, B.L., Schreiber, C.A.
    and Redelmeier, D.A., 1993. When more pain is preferred to less:
    Adding a better end. *Psychological Science*, 4(6), pp.401–405.

34 Corsini, R.J. and Ozaki, B.D., 1994. *Encyclopedia of Psychology*
    (Vol. 1). Wiley.

35 Maslow, A.H. (1964). *Religions, Values, and Peak Experiences*.
    Penguin.

36 Maslow, A. H. (1962). *Toward a Psychology of Being*.
    Princeton, NJ: Van Nostrand-Reinhold.

37 Heath, C. and Heath, D., 2017. *The Power of Moments: Why Certain
    Experiences Have Extraordinary Impact*. Simon and Schuster.

38 Cojuharenco, I. and Ryvkin, D., 2008. Peak–end rule versus
    average utility: how utility aggregation affects evaluations
    of experiences. *Journal of Mathematical Psychology*, 52(5), pp.326–335.

39 Fredrickson, B.L., 2000. Extracting meaning from past affective
    experiences: The importance of peaks, ends, and specific emotions.
    Cognition & Emotion, 14(4), pp.577–606.

40 Schell, J., 2014. *The Art of Game Design: A Book of Lenses*.
    AK Peters/CRC Press.

41 Desmet, P.M. and Pohlmeyer, A.E., 2013. Positive design: An intro-
    duction to design for subjective well-being.
    International Journal of Design, 7(3).

42 Gottman, J.M. and Levenson, R.W., 2000. The timing of divorce:
    Predicting when a couple will divorce over a 14-year period.
    Journal of Marriage and Family, 62(3), pp.737–745.

CHAPTER FOUR: The Myth of Rationality

43   Retrieved from: https://www.meaningful-brands.com/en/our-study

44   Godin, S., March 10th, 2017. On "dating" your customers.
      Nordic Business Forum. Retrieved from: https://www.youtube.com/
      watch?v=IjDJqnQ5G3o

45   Mill, J.S., 1836. On the definition of political economy;
      and on the method of investigation proper to it.
      London and Westminster Review, *4*(October), pp.120–164.

46   Tittenbrun, J., 2013. The death of the economic man.
      International Letters of Social and Humanistic Sciences, (11), pp.10–34.

47   Thaler, R.H., 2000. From homo economicus to homo sapiens.
      Journal of Economic Perspectives, *14*(1), pp.133–141.

48   Tractinsky, N., Katz, A.S. and Ikar, D., 2000. What is beautiful
      is usable. *Interacting with Computers*, *13*(2), pp.127–145.

49   Ariely, D., 2008. *Predictably Irrational*. New York, NY: Harper Audio.

50   Bechara, A., Damasio, H. and Damasio, A.R., 2000. Emotion,
      decision making and the orbitofrontal cortex. *Cerebral Cortex*, *10*(3),
      pp.295–307.

51   Jaffe, M.E., Reutner, L. and Greifeneder, R., 2019. Catalyzing deci-
      sions: How a coin flip strengthens affective reactions.
      PloS One, *14*(8).

52   Gilbert, DT. 2006. *Stumbling on Happiness*. New York, NY: Knopf.

53   Ariely, D., 2008. *Predictably Irrational*. New York, NY: Harper Audio.

54   Barrett, L.F., 2017. *How Emotions are Made: The Secret Life
      of The Brain*. Houghton Mifflin Harcourt.

55   Lerner, J.S., Li, Y., Valdesolo, P. and Kassam, K.S., 2015. Emotion
      and decision making. *Annual Review of Psychology*, *66*, pp.799–823.

CHAPTER FIVE: Basics

56   Hassenzahl, M., 2004. The interplay of beauty, goodness, and usa-
      bility in interactive products. *Human-Computer Interaction*, 19(4),
      pp.319–349.

57   Kano, N., 1984. Attractive quality and must-be quality. Hinshitsu
      Quality, *The Journal of Japanese Society for Quality Control*, 14,
      pp.39–48.

58   Sauerwein, E., Bailom, F., Matzler, K. and Hinterhuber, H.H., 1996.
      The Kano Model: How to delight your customers. In *International
      Working Seminar on Production Economics*
      (Vol. 1, No. 4, pp. 313–327).

59   Johnston, R., 1995. The determinants of service quality: satisfiers
      and dissatisfiers. *International Journal of Service Industry
      Management*, 6(5), pp.53–71.

60   Hassenzahl, M., 2010. Experience design: Technology for all the right
      reasons. *Synthesis Lectures on Human-Centered Informatics*, 3(1),
      pp.1–95.

61   Parasuraman, A., Berry, L.L. and Zeithaml, V.A., 1991. Understanding
      customer expectations of service. *Sloan Management Review*, 32(3),
      pp.39–48.

62   Bevan, N., 1995. Measuring usability as quality of use.
      Software Quality Journal, 4(2), pp.115–130.

63   Schneiderman, B.,1998. *Designing the User Interface*. 3rd edition.
      Addison-Wesley.

64   Hassenzahl, M., 2010. Experience design: Technology for all the right
      reasons. *Synthesis Lectures on Human-Centered Informatics*, 3(1),
      pp.1–95.

65   Hekkert, P., 2006. Design aesthetics: Principles of pleasure
      in design. *Psychology Science*, 48(2), p.157.

66   Hekkert, P. and Leder, H., 2008. Product aesthetics.
      In Product Experience, Elsevier. pp. 259–285.

67   Dewey, J., 2005. *Art as Experience*. Penguin.

68 Pink, D.H., 2005. *A Whole New Mind*. Chautauqua Institution.

69 Seligman, M.E., 1972. Learned helplessness. *Annual Review of Medicine*, *23*(1), pp.407–412.

CHAPTER SIX: Motivators

70 Zimmerman, J., April 2009,. Designing for the self: making products that help people become the person they desire to be. In *Proceedings of the SIGCHI Conference on Human Factors in Computing Systems*, ACM. pp. 395–404.

71 Seligman, M.E. and Csikszentmihalyi, M., 2014. Positive psychology: An introduction. In *Flow and the Foundations of Positive Psychology*. Springer, pp. 279–298.

72 James, W., 2007. *The Principles of Psychology* (Vol. 1). Cosimo, Inc.

73 Parasuraman, A., Berry, L.L. and Zeithaml, V.A., 1991. Understanding customer expectations of service. *Sloan Management Review*, *32*(3), pp.39–48.

74 To read more see: Bloom, P., 2017. *Against Empathy: The Case For Rational Compassion*. Random House.

75 Carroll, J.M., 2004. Beyond fun. *Interactions*, *11*(5), pp.38–40.

76 Carroll, J.M. and Thomas, J.C., 1988. Fun. *ACM SIGCHI Bulletin*, *19*(3), pp.21–24.

77 Valentine experiment gets Danes to show love. *The Local*. 5 February, 2015. Retrieved from: https://www.thelocal.dk/20150205/valentine-experiment-gets-danes-to-show-their-love

78 Zak, P.J., 2006. Love, belief, and neurobiology of attachment. *Loma Linda University, Center for Bioethics*.

79 Schneiderman, B., 2004. Designing for fun: how can we design user interfaces to be more fun? *Interactions*, *11*(5), pp.48–50.

80 Csikszentmihalyi, M., Abuhamdeh, S. and Nakamura, J., 1990. Flow. In A. J. Elliot & C. S. Dweck (Eds.), *Handbook of Competence and Motivation* (p. 598–608). Guilford Publications.

81   Bakker, A.B., Schaufeli, W.B., Leiter, M.P. and Taris, T.W., 2008. Work engagement: An emerging concept in occupational health psychology. *Work & Stress*, 22(3), pp.187–200.

82   Ryan, R.M. and Deci, E.L., 2000. Intrinsic and extrinsic motivations: Classic definitions and new directions. *Contemporary Educational Psychology*, 25(1), pp.54–67.

83   Bucher, A., 2020. *Engaged: Designing for Behavior Change*. Rosenfeld.

84   Sorenson, S. and Adkins, A., 22 July, 2014. Why customer engagement matters so much now: Wary consumers will give more money to the businesses they feel emotionally connected to – while ignoring others. *Gallup Business Journal*. Retrieved from: www.news.gallup.com/businessjournal/172637/why-customer-engagement-matters.aspx

85   Gould, S., 2017. *The Shape of Engagement: The Art of Building Enduring Connections With Your Customers, Employees and Communities.*

86   Mycoskie, B., 20 September, 2011. How I did it: The TOMS story. *Entrepreneur Europe*. Retrieved from: https://www.entrepreneur.com/article/220350

87   Seligman, M.E., 2012. *Flourish: A Visionary New Understanding of Happiness and Well-being..* Simon and Schuster.

88   Diller, S., Shedroff, N. and Rhea, D., 2005. *Making Meaning: How Successful Businesses Deliver Meaningful Customer Experiences.* New Riders.

89   Bucher, A., 2020. *Engaged: Designing for Behavior Change*. Rosenfeld.

90   Rossman, J.R. and Duerden, M.D., 2019. *Designing Experiences*. Columbia University Press.

91   Frankl, V.E., 1985. *Man's Search for Meaning*. Simon and Schuster.

92   *Nicomachean Ethics*—NE—X,6, 1176b 5

93 Seligman, M.E., 2004. *Authentic Happiness: Using The New Positive Psychology To Realize Your Potential For Lasting Fulfillment.* Simon and Schuster.

CHAPTER SEVEN: The Umami of Business

94 Andaleeb, S.S., 1995. Dependence relations and the moderating role of trust: implications for behavioral intentions in marketing channels. *International Journal of Research in Marketing*, 12(2), pp.157–172.

95 Yoon, J., 2018. Escaping the Emotional Blur: Design Tools for Facilitating Positive Emotional Granularity. *Doctoral dissertation, Delft University of Technology.*

96 Damasio, A.R., 2006. *Descartes' Error.* Random House.

97 Barrett, L.F., 2006. Solving the emotion paradox: Categorization and the experience of emotion. *Personality and Social Psychology Review*, 10(1), pp.20–46.

98 Barrett, L.F., 2006. Solving the emotion paradox: Categorization and the experience of emotion. *Personality and Social Psychology Review*, 10(1), pp.20–46.

99 Desmet, P. and Hassenzahl, M., 2012. Towards happiness: Possibility-driven design. In *Human-Computer Interaction: The Agency Perspective* (pp. 3–27). Springer, Berlin, Heidelberg.

100 Diener, E., Suh, E.M., Lucas, R.E. and Smith, H.L., 1999. Subjective well-being: Three decades of progress. *Psychological Bulletin*, 125(2), p.276.

101 Gilmore, J.H. and Pine, B.J., 2007. *Authenticity: What Consumers Really Want.* Harvard Business Press.

102 Diener, E., Suh, E.M., 1999. National differences in subjective well-being. In: Kahneman, D., Diener, E., Schwarz, N. (eds.) *Well-Being: The Foundations of Hedonic Psychology*, Sage, New York, pp. 434–450.

103 King, L.A. and Broyles, S.J., 1997. Wishes, gender, personality, and well-being. *Journal of Personality*, 65(1), pp.49–76.

104 Lyubomirsky, S., 2008. *The How of Happiness: A Scientific Approach To Getting The Life You Want.* Penguin.

105 Diener, E., 1984. Subjective well-being. *Psychological Bulletin*, 95(3), p.542.

106 Desmet, P. and Hassenzahl, M., 2012. Towards happiness: Possibility-driven design. In *Human-Computer Interaction: The Agency Perspective*. Springer, pp. 3–27.

107 Vallerand, R.J., 2000. Deci and Ryan's self-determination theory: A view from the hierarchical model of intrinsic and extrinsic motivation. *Psychological Inquiry*, 11(4), pp.312–318.

108 The drawing at the end of this chapter is adapted from the model proposed by Pieter Desmet, a Professor at the Delft Institute of Positive Design (diopd.org).

PART II: Building Umami Strategy

CHAPTER ONE: The Danger of Playing It Safe

109 Godin, S., 2009. *Purple Cow, New Edition: Transform Your Business By Being Remarkable*. Penguin.

110 Godin, S., 2009. *Purple Cow, New Edition: Transform Your Business By Being Remarkable*. Penguin.

111 Pine, B.J., Pine, J. and Gilmore, J.H., 1999. *The Experience Economy: Work is Theatre & Every Business a Stage*. Harvard Business Press.

112 Schwartz, B., 2004, January. *The Paradox of Choice: Why More is Less*. New York: Ecco.

113 Moon, Y., 2010. Different: *Escaping the Competitive Herd*. Crown Business.

114 Kotter, J., 30 January, 2020. Beware of Benchmarking and Best Practices. *Forbes*. Retrieved from: www.forbes.com/sites/johnkotter/2020/01/30/beware-of-benchmarking-and-best-practices/#3c0d97205293

115 Collins, J.C., Collins, J. and Porras, J.I., 2005. *Built to Last: Successful Habits of Visionary Companies*. Random House.

116 Grant, R.M., 2016. *Contemporary Strategy Analysis: Text and Cases*. John Wiley & Sons.

117 Gelles, D. Kitroeff, N., Nicas, J., and Ruiz, R.R., 23 March, 2019. Boeing was 'Go, Go, Go" to beat Airbus with 737 Max. *New York Times*. Retrieved from: https://www.nytimes.com/2019/03/23/business/boeing-737-max-crash.html?module=inline

118 The differentiation visualisation is borrowed from Moon, Y., 2010. *Different: Escaping the Competitive Herd*. Crown Business.

CHAPTER TWO: The Umami Baseline

119 Reeves, B. and Nass, C.I., 1996. *The Media Equation: How People Treat Computers, Television, and New Media Like Real People and Places*. Cambridge University Press.

120 Bruner, J.S., 1990. *Acts of Meaning (Vol. 3)*. Harvard University Press.

121 Whyte Jr, W.H., 1954. The web of word of mouth. *Fortune*, 50(5), pp.140–143.

122 Engel, J.F., Kegerreis, R.J. and Blackwell, R.D., 1969. Word of mouth communication by the innovator. *Journal of Marketing*, 33(3), pp.15–19.

123 Anderson, E.W., 1998. Customer satisfaction and word of mouth. *Journal of Service Research*, 1(1), pp.5–17.

124 Schutz, A., 1996. The problem of social reality. In *Collected Papers*. Springer, pp. 71–72.

125 Berger, J., 2013. *Contagious: Why Things Catch On*. Simon and Schuster.

126 Schmitt, P., Skiera, B. and Van den Bulte, C., 2011. Referral programs and customer value. *Journal of Marketing*, 75(1), pp.46–59.

127 Keller, E. and Fay, B., 2012. *The Face-to-Face Book: Why Real Relationships Rule in a Digital Marketplace*. Simon and Schuster.

128 Reason, B., Løvlie, L. and Flu, M., 2015. *Service Design for Business*. Wiley.

129 Plutchik, R., 1991. *The Emotions*. University Press of America.

130   For more information see: 21 March, 2020. Putting some emotion
      into your design – Plutchik's Wheel of Emotions.
      Interaction Design Foundation. Retrieved from: https://
      www.interaction-design.org/literature/article/
      putting-some-emotion-into-your-design-plutchik-s-wheel-of-emotions

131   Van der Merwe, S.E., Biggs, R., Preiser, R., Cunningham, C.,
      Snowden, D.J., O'Brien, K., Jenal, M., Vosloo, M., Blignaut, S.
      and Goh, Z., 2019. Making sense of complexity: using SenseMaker
      as a research tool. *Systems*, 7(2), p.25.

132   Friedman, M., 13 September, 1970. In a free-enterprise: A Friedman
      doctrine – the social responsibility of business is to increase its prof-
      its. *New York Times Magazine.* Retrieved from: https://www.nytimes.
      com/1970/09/13/archives/a-friedman-doctrine-the-social-responsi-
      bility-of-business-is-to.html

133   In an interview by Simon Sinek with Jeff Immelt cited in the book
      Sinek, S., 2019. The Infinite Game. Portfolio/Penguin.

CHAPTER THREE: Umami Vision

134   Frankl, V.E., 1985. *Man's Search for Meaning.* Simon and Schuster.

135   Levitt, T., 1960. *Marketing Myopia.* London: Boston.

136   Sinek, S., 2009. *Start with Why: How Great Leaders Inspire Everyone
      To Take Action.* Penguin.

137   Collins, J., 2016. *Good to Great: Why Some Companies Make The Leap
      and Others Don't.* Instaread.

138   Sinek, S., 2009. *Start with Why: How Great Leaders Inspire Everyone
      To Take Action.* Penguin.

139   Sinek, S., 2019. *The Infinite Game.* Penguin.

140   This list is inspired by the Clearing Purpose Framework
      proposed by Joana Mao, (http://clearpurpose.global).

141   https://eu.patagonia.com/gb/en/company-info.html

142   Sinek, S., 2019. *The Infinite Game.* Penguin.

143 Chen, M.J. and Miller, D., 2011. The relational perspective as a business mindset: Managerial implications for East and West. *Academy of Management Perspectives*, 25(3), pp.6–18.

144 Lovallo, D. and Sibony, O., 2010. The case for behavioral strategy. *McKinsey Quarterly*, 2(1), pp.30–43.

145 tylko.com

146 Haque, U., 2011. *Betterness: Economics For Humans.* Harvard Business Review Press.

147 Stephens, G.J., Silbert, L.J. and Hasson, U., 2010. Speaker–listener neural coupling underlies successful communication. *Proceedings of the National Academy of Sciences*, 107(32), pp.14425–14430.

148 Seaman Jr. J.T., and Smith G.D., December 2012. Your company's history as a leadership tool. *Harvard Business Review*. Retrieved from: https://hbr.org/2012/12/your-companys-history-as-a-leadership-tool

149 Davis J., 4 June, 2017. How Lego clicked: the super brand that reinvented itself. *Guardian*. Retrieved from: https://www.theguardian.com/lifeandstyle/2017/jun/04/how-lego-clicked-the-super-brand-that-reinvented-itself

150 Robertson, D. and Breen, B., 2014. *Brick by Brick: How LEGO Rewrote the Rules of Innovation and Conquered the Global Toy Industry.* Crown Business.

151 James, W., 2007. *The Principles of Psychology (Vol. 1)*. Cosimo, Inc..

152 Goffman, E., 1978. *The Presentation of Self in Everyday Life* (p. 56). London: Harmondsworth.

153 Wells, W.D., 1975. Psychographics: A critical review. *Journal of Marketing Research*, 12(2), pp.196–213.

154 Wells, W.D. ed., 2011. *Life Style and Psychographics (Chapter 13): Life Style and Psychographics: Definitions, Uses, and Problems.* Marketing Classics Press.

CHAPTER FOUR: Umami Edges

155   Malcolm Campbell talks about the ancient Nordic concept
      of Seidr in an interview on the Catching the Next Wave podcast.
      Retrieved from: https://catchingthenextwave.simplecast.com/
      episodes/508-malcolm-campbell

156   Godin, S., 2009. *Purple Cow, New Edition: Transform Your Business By
      Being Remarkable*. Penguin.

157   Lloyd, C., 16 January, 2018. How to buy stuff at
      the Apple store without a cashier. *How–To Geek*.
      Retrieved from: www.howtogeek.com/338754/
      how-to-buy-stuff-at-the-apple-store-without-a-cashier/

158   Morgan, A. and Barden, M., 2015. *A Beautiful Constraint:
      How to Transform Your Limitations into Advantages,
      and Why It's Everyone's Business*. John Wiley & Sons.

159   Gould, S.J., 1980. The Evolutionary Biology of Constraint.
      Daedalus, pp.39–52.

160   Smith, O., 20 September, 2018. Revolut's Nikolay Storonsky
      is building the Amazon of banking. *Forbes*. Retrieved from:
      https://www.forbes.com/sites/oliversmith/2018/09/20/revo-
      luts-nikolay-storonsky-is-building-the-amazon-of-banking/#59e-
      c622118a9

161   Bianchini, F., 1993. Culture, conflict and cities: issues and prospects
      for the 1990s. *Cultural Policy and Urban Regeneration:
      The West European experience*, pp.199–213.

162   Matarasso, F. and Landry, C., 1999. Balancing Act: twenty-one
      strategic dilemmas in cultural policy (Vol. 4). *Council of Europe*.

CHAPTER FIVE: Umami Metrics

163   George, R., 2011. *The Big Necessity: Adventures In The World
      of Human Waste*. Portobello Books.

164   Gilb, T., 2006. Evolutionary project management: Multiple per-
      formance, quality and cost metrics for early and continuous
      stakeholder value delivery. In *Enterprise Information Systems VI*,
      Springer, pp. 24–29..

165 https://www.gatesfoundation.org/How-We-Work/Quick-Links/Grants-Database/Grants/2013/07/OPP1083134

166 Hubbard, D.W., 2014. *How to Measure Anything: Finding the Value of Intangibles in Business.* John Wiley & Sons.

167 Posavac, S.S., Kardes, F.R. and Brakus, J.J., 2010. Focus induced tunnel vision in managerial judgment and decision making: The peril and the antidote. *Organizational Behavior and Human Decision Processes, 113*(2), pp.102–111.

168 Kahneman, D. and Henik, A., 2017. Perceptual organization and attention. In *Perceptual Organization,* Routledge, pp. 181–211.

169 www.gilb.com

170 Similar to what OKRs (Objective-Key Results) promise. To find out more about OKRs see: Doerr, J., 2018. *Measure What Matters: How Google, Bono, and the Gates Foundation Rock The World with OKRs,* Penguin.

PART III: Keeping the Umami Mindset

CHAPTER ONE: Positive Adaptation

171 Brickman, P., Coates, D. and Janoff-Bulman, R., 1978. Lottery winners and accident victims: Is happiness relative?
Journal of Personality and Social Psychology, 36(8), p.917.

172 Di Tella, R., Haisken-De New, J. and MacCulloch, R., 2010. Happiness adaptation to income and to status in an individual panel.
Journal of Economic Behavior & Organization, 76(3), pp.834–852.

173 Boswell, W.R., Boudreau, J.W. and Tichy, J., 2005. The relationship between employee job change and job satisfaction: the honey-moon-hangover effect. *Journal of Applied Psychology, 90*(5), p.882.

174 Kahneman, D., 1999. Objective happiness. *Well-being: The Foundations of Hedonic Psychology, 3*(25), pp.1–23.

175 Brey, P., Briggle, A. and Spence, E. eds., 2012. *The Good Life in a Technological Age.* Routledge.

176   Lyubomirsky, S., Dickerhoof, R., Boehm, J.K. and Sheldon, K.M.,
      2011. Becoming happier takes both a will and a proper way:
      An experimental longitudinal intervention to boost well-being.
      Emotion, 11(2), p.391.

177   Pohlmeyer, A.E., 2017. How design can (not) support human flour-
      ishing. In *Positive Psychology Interventions in Practice,*
      Springer, pp. 235–255.

178   Van Boven, L., 2005. Experientialism, materialism, and the pursuit
      of happiness. *Review of General Psychology*, 9(2), pp.132–142.

179   Frederick, S. and Loewenstein, G., 1999. 16 Hedonic adaptation.
      Well-being: The Foundations of Hedonic Psychology, pp.302–329.

180   Chouinard, Y., 2016. *Let My People Go Surfing: The Education
      of a Reluctant Businessman – Including 10 More Years of Business
      Unusual*. Penguin.

181   Data retrieved from the Environmental Impact of the Textile
      and Clothing Industry: What Consumers Need to Know. *Report
      by European Parliament Think Tank*, 17-01-2019. Retrieved from:
      https://www.europarl.europa.eu/thinktank/en/document.
      html?reference=EPRS_BRI(2019)633143

182   Perry, P., 8 January, 2018. The environmental cost of fast fashion.
      The Independent. Retrieved from: www.independent.co.uk/life-style/
      fashion/environment-costs-fast-fashion-pollution-waste-sustainabili-
      ty-a8139386.html

183   Chouinard, Y. and Stanley, V., 2013. *The Responsible Company:
      What We've Learned from Patagonia's First 40 years*. Patagonia.

184   Bloomfield, K., 21 December, 2018. Monzo: The rise and rise
      of the coolest challenger in the class. *The Finch Times*. Retrieved
      from: https://thefintechtimes.com/monzo-challenger/

185   Myerson, R.B., 2013. *Game Theory*. Harvard University Press.

CHAPTER TWO: The Infinite Game

186   Carse, J., 2011. *Finite and Infinite Games*. Simon and Schuster.

187   Haque, U., 2011. *The New Capitalist Manifesto: Building a Disruptively
      Better Business*. Harvard Business Press.

188 Haque, U. 31 July, 2009. The value every business needs
     to create now. *Harvard Business Review*. Retrieved from:
     https://hbr.org/2009/07/the-value-every-business-needs

189 Moore, G.A. and McKenna, R., 1999. *Crossing the Chasm*.
     HarperCollins Publishers.

190 Nunes, P., and Breene, T. 2011. Reinvent your business before it's
     too late. *Harvard Business Review 89, no. 1/2:* 80–87. Retrieved from:
     https://hbr.org/2011/01/reinvent-your-business-before-its-too-late

191 Snowden, D., 8 July, 2016. Thinking flexuously. *Cognitive Edge Blog*.
     Retrieved from: http://cognitive-edge.com/blog/thinking-flexuously/

192 https://www.britannica.com/sports/skiing

193 Jans, G., 28 January, 2018. Rossignol wants to become an all-
     year brand: "This is a sea change for the Rossignol Group"
     – an interview with Rossignol Group CEO Bruno Cercley. *ispo.
     com*. Retrieved from: https://www.ispo.com/en/companies/
     rossignol-wants-become-all-year-brand

194 Carse, J., 2011. *Finite and Infinite Games*. Simon and Schuster.

195 Sinek, S., 2019. *The Infinite Game*. Penguin.

196 Keiningham, T.L., Aksoy, L., Cooil, B., Andreassen, T.W.
     and Williams, L., 2008. A holistic examination of Net Promoter.
     Journal of Database Marketing & Customer Strategy Management,
     15(2), pp.79–90.

CHAPTER THREE: Moving Forward in Times of Complexity

197 Snowden D.J., and Boone, M.E., November 2007. A leader's frame-
     work for decision making. *Harvard Business Review*. Retrieved from:
     https://hbr.org/2007/11/a-leaders-framework-for-decision-making

198 Kurtz, C.F. and Snowden, D.J., 2003. The new dynamics of strategy:
     Sense-making in a complex and complicated world.
     IBM Systems Journal, 42(3), pp.462–483.

199 Kurtz, C.F. and Snowden, D.J., 2003. The new dynamics of strategy:
     Sense-making in a complex and complicated world.
     IBM Systems Journal, 42(3), pp.462–483.

200 Standish Group, Chaos Studies, 2013–2017.
Retrieved from: https://vitalitychicago.com/blog/
agile-projects-are-more-successful-traditional-projects/

201 Dawkins, R., 2016. *The Selfish Gene*. Oxford University Press.

202 Tetlock, P.E. and Gardner, D., 2016. *Superforecasting:
The Art and Science of Prediction*. Random House.

203 More about inspect-and-adapt practice can be found in Reis,
E., 2011. *The Lean Startup*. New York: Crown Business.

204 Snowden, D. Safe-to-fail probes. Cognitive Edge Blog. Retrieved
from: https://cognitive-edge.com/methods/safe-to-fail-probes/

205 Holmquist, L.E., 2012. *Grounded Innovation: Strategies For Creating
Digital Products*. Elsevier.

206 Bell, M.S., 2000. *Narrative Design: Working with Imagination, Craft,
and Form*, WW Norton & Company.

207 Gaver, B. and Martin, H., April 2000. Alternatives: exploring
information appliances through conceptual design proposals.
In *Proceedings of the SIGCHI Conference on Human Factors
in Computing Systems*, pp. 209–216.

208 Marzano, R.J., Pickering, D. and Pollock, J.E., 2001. *Classroom
Instruction That Works: Research-based Strategies for Increasing Student
Achievement*. ASCD.

209 Stappers P. J. and Giaccardi E. *Research through Design*.
The Encyclopedia of Human-Computer Interaction, 2nd Edition.
Retreived from: https://www.interaction-design.org/literature/
book/the-encyclopedia-of-human-computer-interaction-2nd-ed/
research-through-design

210 Gaver, W., Boucher, A., Law, A., Pennington, S., Bowers, J., Beaver,
J., Humble, J., Kerridge, T., Villar, N. and Wilkie, A., April 2008.
Threshold devices: looking out from the home. In *Proceedings
of the SIGCHI Conference on Human Factors in Computing Systems*,
pp. 1429–1438.

211 Gaver, W., 2012, May. What should we expect from research
through design? In *Proceedings of the SIGCHI Conference on Human
Factors in Computing Systems*, pp. 937–946.

212 Piaget, J., 1972. Development and learning.
     Readings on the Development of Children, pp.25–33.

213 Frayling, C. (1993). Research in art and design.
     Royal College of Art Research Papers series, 1(1).

214 Jonas, W. (2007b). Research through DESIGN through research:
     A cybernetic model of designing design foundations. *Kybernetes,
     36*(9/10), 1362–1380.

215 Zimmerman, J., Stolterman, E., & Forlizzi, J. (2010). An analysis
     and critique of Research through Design: towards a formalization
     of a research approach. Paper presented at the *Designing Interactive
     Systems*, Aarhus, Denmark.

216 Kay, J., January 17, 2004. *Obliquity*. John Kay Blog. Retrieved from:
     https://www.johnkay.com/2004/01/17/obliquity/

217 Snowden, D., 21 August, 2015. Change through small actions
     in the present. *Cognitive Edge Blog*. Retrieved from: https://cogni-
     tive-edge.com/blog/change-through-small-actions-in-the-present/

CHAPTER FOUR: The Magic of Underpromising

218 Eisner, M., 1998. *Work in Progress*. Random House.

219 Vieth, M.D., 2009. Commitments and Reciprocity in Trust Situations:
     Experimental studies on obligation, indignation, and self-consistency.
     Utrecht University.

220 Peters, T., 1987. Under promise, over deliver. Retrieved from:
     https://tompeters.com/columns/under-promise-over-deliver/

221 Oliver, R.L., 1980. A cognitive model of the antecedents and con-
     sequences of satisfaction decisions. *Journal of Marketing Research,
     17*(4), pp.460–469.

222 Arora, N., 24 January, 2013. Apple kicks Jobs' UPOD strategy
     to the curb in Cupertino. *Forbes*. Retrieved from:
     https://www.forbes.com/sites/greatspeculations/2013/01/24/apple-
     kicks-jobs-upod-strategy-to-the-curb-in-cupertino/#14d414975a12

223   Kalb, I., 19 March, 2013. Steve Jobs used a simple rule to make peo-
      ple fall in love with Apple products. *Business Insider.* Retrieved from:
      https://www.businessinsider.com/the-lost-art-of-marketing-technolo-
      gy-underpromising-and-overdelivering-2013-3?IR=T

224   Feng, J. and Papatla, P., 2011. Advertising: stimulant or suppressant
      of online word of mouth? *Journal of Interactive Marketing,* 25(2),
      pp.75–84.

225   Hogan, J.E., Lemon, K.N. and Libai, B., 2004. Quantifying the ripple:
      Word-of-mouth and advertising effectiveness. *Journal of Advertising
      Research,* 44(3), pp.271–280.

CHAPTER FIVE: The Inevitability of Resistance

226   Pressfield, S., 2002. *The War of Art: Break Through The Blocks
      and Win Your Inner Creative Battles..* Black Irish Entertainment LLC.

227   Godin, S., 2007. *The Dip: A Little Book that Teaches You When to Quit
      (and When to Stick).* Penguin.

228   Godin, S., 2007. *The Dip: A Little Book that Teaches You When to Quit
      (and When to Stick).* Penguin.

229   Zipf, G.K., 1932. *Selected Studies of The Principle of Relative Frequency
      in Language.* Harvard University Press.

230   Pfanner, E., 21 May, 2007. Zipf's Law, or the considerable value
      of being top dog, as applied to branding. *New York Times.* Retrieved
      from: https://www.nytimes.com/2007/05/21/business/21zipf.html

231   Brown, J., 2006. Reflective practices for transformational leaders.
      FutureAge, 5(3), pp.6–9.

Afterword

232   Geek Squad offers their repair services not only online, but also
      in-store and at-home. All employees are dressed a little like
      Will Smith in *Men in Black* and they drive characteristic Priuses
      called *Geekmobiles.*